Professionalism and the Public Interest

I0129061

MIT Press Series in Health and Public Policy
Jeffrey E. Harris, general editor

1. *Professionalism and the Public Interest: Price and Quality in Optometry*, James W. Begun, 1981.

Professionalism and the Public Interest

Price and Quality in Optometry

James W. Begun

The MIT Press
Cambridge, Massachusetts, and London, England

This book was set in VIP Palatino by Grafacon Inc. and printed and bound
by The Murray Printing Company in the United States of America.

Library of Congress Cataloging in Publication Data

Begun, James W
  Professionalism and the public interest.

  (MIT series in health and public policy; 1)
  Bibliography: p.
  Includes index.
    1. Optometry—United   States.   I. Title.   II. Series: Massachusetts
Institute of Technology.   MIT series in health and public policy;
1. [DNLM: 1. Optometry—Standards. 2. Professional competence.
3. Fees and charges.   4.   Quality of health care.
WW721 B418p]
RE959.B43   617.7′5′023   80-22570
ISBN 0-262-02156-0

MIT Press

0262021560

BEGUN
PROF PUBLIC INT

Contents

List of Tables

Series Foreword

This MIT Press series will serve as a forum for significant new research in the field of health and public policy. The series will encompass current problems in health-care organization, financing, and regulation. It will also focus on emerging policy problems in environmental health, workplace safety, toxic substances, and the assessment of new medical technology. We plan to publish original scholarly monographs, highly focused collections by multiple authors, and textbooks that explore new fields.

This volume by James W. Begun of Cornell University explores the central questions in public policy toward the health-care professions: Should our society continue to grant self-regulating autonomy to the health professions? Does professional protection guarantee higher quality service? Or is professionalism a privilege exploited for self-interest? Professor Begun's research focuses on professionalism in optometry. But his work has larger application to the entire health-care field.

Jeffrey E. Harris

Preface

My Ph.D. dissertation, submitted in 1977 to the Department of Sociology, University of North Carolina at Chapel Hill, served as the stimulus for this book. Several faculty members helped me with my work. Duncan MacRae, Jr., introduced me to the area of policy analysis and rendered painstaking and perceptive criticisms of the dissertation. For several years Patricia Rieker and Gordon DeFriese have provided encouragement and insightful criticisms, and Gordon stimulated my interest in optometry and furnished a supportive working environment in the Health Services Research Center. The original proposal for this study benefited from the encouragement and comments of Lee Benham. Richard Simpson, Arnold Kaluzny, and Roger Feldman contributed useful suggestions to earlier drafts of this document.

Without the financial support of the National Center for Health Services Research, Office of the Assistant Secretary for Health, DHEW, this work would not have been possible. Support was furnished by grant numbers HS-02371 (in 1976–77) and HS-03085 (in 1978–79). Additionally, the research would not have been possible without the encouragement and cooperation of optometrists. The American Optometric Association afforded access to a wealth of information on historical and current issues. The International Association of Boards of Examiners in Optometry (IAB) assisted in gaining access to optometric officials and supplied a cover letter for a national survey of optometrists. In particular, John Robinson of the IAB gave freely of his time to assist this research. Numerous optometrists, who shall remain anonymous, gave interviews and comments in the process of my work, and over a thousand took the time to respond to a national questionnaire survey.

I found the professionals surprisingly and pleasingly open-minded; they were frank and revealing in their conversations with me despite recent criticism from researchers, state and federal agencies, and congressional committees. They are criticized at times in this work too, but I encourage them to remain as receptive and open to scrutiny as I have found them to be.

Part of the work on this book was conducted while I was on the faculty of the Department of Social and Administrative Medicine, School of Medicine, University of North Carolina at Chapel Hill. I appreciate the encouragement to pursue my research interests given by the department chairperson, Glenn Wilson. Finally, I wish to thank the following individuals for their contributions to the preparation of this book: Anne Begun, Lynn Black, Ed Crowe, Nita Ingram, Phyllis Johnson, Priscilla Kistler, Ron Lippincott, John Mann, W. Earl Mitchelle, and Terri Sullivan.

Public Policy and the Professions

In the United States the term *professionalism* has traditionally referred to the provision of expert, high quality service to the consumer—the goal of all occupational groups. Members of the established and aspiring professions in particular are supportive of this definition. In the minds of many citizens today, however, professionalism is a word that connotes elitism, exclusion, and exploitation. Professions are seen as grasping, careless elite groups responsible to no one, rather than altruistic groups of experts whose ethics ensure the quality of their services at a fair price.

The philosophy of professionalism rests on the assumption that in return for a privilege—autonomy from direct societal control—professions will deliver services at prices that do not exploit the privilege of self-regulation. This assumed attribute of professionals most commonly is referred to as a service orientation—a manner of behaving in which dedication to a client's interest takes precedence over personal profit when the two happen to come into conflict (Bledstein, 1976:87). Professions serve the public interest. However, others argue that professionalism results in personal gain for members of an occupation, and thus professionals primarily serve their own self-interest. These two perspectives provide the basis for the societal debate over professionalism.

The Growth of Professionalism in the United States

The degree to which professions serve the public interest is an issue of increasing importance as occupations continue to specialize and professionalize. In recent U.S. history occupations typically have tried to professionalize by developing a full-time occupation, training schools, a national association, legal recognition, and a code of ethics (Wilensky, 1964). A profession is an occupation whose elevated status has been recognized by society, often by licensure laws that grant the privilege of self-regulation. Professions commonly claim possession of certain attributes that mere "occupations" do not possess. These attributes include commitment to the occupation, high educational attainment, and a service orientation. The profession may or may not possess these attributes; what is important is that society believes that the occupation possesses professional attributes.

Today, almost every occupation attempts to attain the label of "professional." Recent articles analyze the professionalization efforts of such diverse groups as personnel managers, occupational therapists, computer programmers, speech pathologists, life underwriters, broadcast newsmen, and conservative rabbis (see Timperly and Osbaldeston, 1975; Bell and Bell, 1972; Nicolais, 1976; Stern and Klock, 1975; Kraft and Weinberg, 1975; Weinthal and O'Keefe, 1974; Zelizer and Zelizer, 1973).

This trend has been identified as a characteristic not only of the United States but of all modern societies. Parsons (1968:536) has written that the development of the professions is probably the most important change that has occurred in the occupational system of modern societies. Goode (1960:902) has suggested that "an industrializing society is a professionalizing society," and the rise of professions in modern societies has led one sociologist to speculate on "The Professionalization of Everyone?" (Wilensky, 1964). Because of the American tradition of limited governmental interference in individual activities and of pluralism in government, the United States in particular among industrialized societies has permitted the development of specialized, expert occupational groupings that have the responsibility for regulating themselves.

Professionalism as a Public-Policy Problem

Until recently the growth of professionalism in the United States has been viewed benignly and has proceeded almost without opposition. Today, however, professionalism has come to be perceived as a public-policy problem by state and federal government.

Since licensing of occupations is a state responsibility and most aspiring professions seek licensing laws, state governments have reason to be concerned about the growth of professionalism. In 1973, it was estimated that the average number of occupations subject to licensure in each state was 39, covering some 307 different occupations (Martin, 1979). State governments are exhibiting more concern over the possible manipulation of self-regulation by the professions, as exhibited by the passage of "sunset" laws in over one-half the states. These laws decree that specified agencies terminate at a particular date unless recreated by new legislation, thus putting the burden of proof for justifying their existence on the agencies. State governments are also conducting other types of independent inquiries into their licensing systems (Halstead, 1975; Baughcum, 1976). Now many states are requiring the appointment of nonprofessional or lay members to licensing boards; in California, for example, the medical board has one-third lay membership.

Much of the public-policy concern over licensing boards is based on the relationships between professional associations and the state licensing boards that regulate the professions. Gilb (1966) presents strong anecdotal evidence on the close linkages between professional associations and state licensing boards, and Akers (1968) documents several similar examples in five health professions in Kentucky. State licensure is viewed by some policy-makers as a "political process critical to the organizational autonomy and self-regulation" of professions, "often promoted as a way to enhance the status and the public image of the group . . . [and] the economic benefit that often accompanies licensure" (Cohen, 1973a; Shimberg et al., 1973:13).

The federal governnent is also showing more inclination to interfere in the previously autonomous functioning of state regulatory boards. For example, the Equal Employment Opportunity Commission (EEOC) has proposed that all licensing, certification and accrediting agencies be required to submit evidence of the validity, relevance and fairness of examinations. The EEOC is attempting to define licensing boards as "employment agencies" because they control entry to the professions (Rose, 1977; Hubbard, 1977).

The Antitrust Division of the U.S. Department of Justice, declaring that state licensing laws "limit competitive freedom, and frequently are used as an affirmative protection by those already permitted into the protected occupation," also intends to be concerned with the professional regulation issue for some time to come (Sims, 1975). The Division has promised to be watchful for attempts of state licensing boards to use regulations as a "convenient cover under which private parties develop, maintain and enforce fundamental competitive restraints . . ." (Wall Street Journal, 1976:4). This view was reflected in a 1977 Supreme Court ruling that struck down legal and ethical bans against the advertising of lawyers' prices and services (*Bates v. State Bar of Arizona*), and the 1975 *Goldfarb v. Virginia State Bar* decision that invalidated minimum fee schedules used by bar associations.

Another federal agency active in the area of professional regulation is the Federal Trade Commission (FTC). In its recent actions, the FTC attempted to preempt state licensing laws regulating pharmacists, opticians, optometrists, and funeral directors, and began investigations of dental, legal, accounting, real estate, and veterinary services (Clarkson and Muris, 1979). In a statement with far-reaching implications, FTC chairman Michael Pertschuk claimed that "More and more we are discovering that professionals are not markedly different from any other sellers who offer their services in trade" (FTC News, 1979a). The equating of professional services with other occupational services, of course, is a threat to the very concept of professionalism.

Professionalism and the Delivery of Health Services

Because their work is technical and specialized, health occupations are particularly good candidates for professionalization. Their services are also important to the physical and mental well-being of the consumer, facilitating a strong public-interest argument for maintaining minimum quality levels. A rapid increase in professionalizing occupations has in fact been characteristic of the field of health care, for the number of specialized health occupations has continued to multiply with the expansion of health knowledge and technology. Between 1968 and 1977, the number of health occupation job titles grew from 375 to 717 (U.S. DHEW, 1970; 1979). Recent years have seen state government licensure of such groups as acupuncturists, clinical laboratory technicians, emergency medical personnel, physician's assistants, radiology technicians, and medical social workers (U.S. DHEW, 1977; Bernstein, 1977). As a result, the largest single concentration of licensed occupations is in the health industry (White, 1979:14).

In spite of, or perhaps because of, the tremendous growth of professionalism in the field of health, the public spirit of cynicism about professionalism extends into the health professions. The 1970s were a decade in which government expressed increasing distrust of the health professions, as reflected in numerous public policies.

National Standards for Health Occupations

In response to the burgeoning number of new health occupations, the Department of Health, Education and Welfare (DHEW) has proposed that national standards be developed for licensing and certifying health occupations (U.S. DHEW, 1976b). The plan was issued following DHEW's recommended moratorium on further state licensing of new health occupations between 1971 and 1975. The Department asserts that the issue to license or not to license is settled in state legislatures based upon the political strengths of the participants rather than public need. The proposal recommends a national certification council to oversee private and state organizations in the health occupation licensing field and to move toward national standards for licensing and certification.

Sunset Commissions
Licensing boards for the health professions typically fall under the jurisdiction of state sunset commissions, but so far there is little experience on which to judge their potential impact on the professions. Since sunset laws resulted from the deregulation movement, it is likely that changes, if any, will be in the direction of decreasing professional power. In North Carolina, for instance, the sunset commission staff in 1979 recommended: the abolition of the opticians' licensing board; decreased regulatory powers for the optometry board; less stringent entry restrictions on out-of-state dentists; and lay members on the optometric and dental boards (N.C. Governmental Evaluation Commission, 1979a–c). Most of the proposals have been strenuously opposed by the affected professions, mainly based upon the potential dilution in the quality of care.

State legislatures were beginning to consider or pass laws challenging professionalism in health before sunset commissions existed, and they continue to do so. In the area of dentistry, for instance, 14 states had bills to legalize denturism pending at the end of 1977, and two states had legalized denturism (Abrams, 1978). Denturism involves the sale of dentures by dental lab technicians directly to consumers, and in competition with dentists. Many states are moving more vigirously to investigate consumer complaints of health providers, particularly physicians (MWN, 1974b), and state laws requiring lay membership on professional licensing boards are proliferating. As a final example, the California State Health Department has proposed new rules that would allow physician's assistants, nurse practitioners, and nurse midwives to prescribe medication, order laboratory tests, and determine therapy in the hospital setting without medical supervision (PEN, 1980). The move is strongly opposed by the medical profession.

The Federal Trade Commission

The Federal Trade Commission (FTC) has moved vigorously against elements of laws and ethical codes that in the FTC's opinion restrict competition within the health professions. In 1975, the FTC proposed rules that would preempt state pharmacist licensing laws restricting prescription drug price advertising (U.S. FTC, 1975). After extensive hearings, the drug rules were abandoned because of a 1976 U.S. Supreme Court decision (*Virginia State Board of Pharmacy v. Virginia Citizens Consumer Council, Inc.*) that allowed drug price advertising under the first amendment to the U.S. Constitution. Similar FTC proposals were made against restrictions on eyeglass advertising (U.S. FTC, 1976a). After a thorough investigation, the Commission unanimously accepted a trade regulation rule which preempts state laws and private ethical codes that prohibit the advertising of prescription eyewear or eye examinations. Affected by the rule are optometrists, opticians, and ophthalmologists. The rule, which became effective July 3, 1978, also requires that consumers be provided with copies of their prescriptions after they have their eyes examined (Federal Register, 1978).

In addition, the FTC in 1975 filed an antitrust complaint against the American Medical Association (AMA), alleging that advertising restrictions in physicians' codes of ethics illegally restrain competition. In late 1978 an administrative law judge's decision supported the FTC's stance; that decision is now under appeal. A similar complaint against the American Dental Association (ADA) will be settled by the AMA decision (FTC News, 1979b).

A recent FTC staff study has charged that physicians tend to bill more for services covered by Blue Shield insurance in which physicians control administration of the plans, and the staff is pursuing evidence of "concerted efforts among providers to frustrate cost-control initiatives sponsored by insurance companies" (Palmer, 1979:279). In another area, the FTC is investigating claims that some health maintenance organizations have been victimized by anticompetitive conduct of fee-for-service physicians. The FTC has challenged relative value fee schedules on the basis that they are used to fix prices, and in 1976 after FTC action two specialty societies (orthopedic surgeons and obstetrician/gynecologists) agreed to abandon relative value scales. A related consent order barred the American Society of Anesthesiology (ASA) from restraining anesthesiologists from working on a salaried, rather than fee-for-service, basis (Palmer, 1979). Finally in the medical area, the

FTC in 1976 commenced an investigation of the control of the supply of health personnel by organized medicine (Avellone and Moore, 1978).

In the field of dental care, the FTC is investigating restrictions on the ability of nondentists to provide denture care directly to the public, the ability of dental hygienists to offer preventive services directly, and several other controls over less traditional types of dental practice (Daynard et al., 1979). Many of these same issues were raised in a recent report by a Council of State Governments task force on state dental policies, again reflecting substantial pressures to loosen restrictions on professional dental practice (COSG, 1979).

The FTC's venture into the health care industry is likely to continue in the immediate future; indeed, its breadth is expanding. In 1977 the FTC sponsored an exploratory national conference on competition in the health sector (Greenberg, 1978) and in 1979 staff members prepared a wide-ranging review of possible initiatives in health services (U.S. FTC, 1979). Such possibilities include investigations of competition among hospitals, physician opposition to the development of nonphysician providers, the unavailability of third-party reimbursement to nurse-practitioners and other nonphysician providers, and patient access to medical records.

Other Attacks on Professionalism in Health

Several other governmental policies have challenged the assumption that all is right with professionalism. The Professional Standards Review Organization (PSRO) law of 1972 mandates physician review of federally-financed inpatient hospital utilization and is meant as both a cost and quality control measure. The movement to establish PSROs clearly was aided by an expanding distrust of the ability of professionals to police themselves adequately (U.S. DHEW, 1972). The law still recognizes a traditional concept of professionalism, however, as nonprofessionals do not participate in PSRO decisions.

The Justice Department, Department of Labor, General Accounting Office (GAO), and the courts are likely to provide support for the general policy of deregulation and heightened competition among health services providers (Sims, 1978; Shimberg, 1979). Since 1975, for example, the Justice Department has filed antitrust suits against the promulgation of relative value scales by associations of podiatrists, anesthesiologists, radiologists, and other health professionals. As mentioned earlier, the Supreme Court, in the 1976 Virginia State Board of Pharmacy decision, overturned legal and ethical restrictions on advertising by pharmacists, and similar decisions by lower courts are multiplying.[1] Finally, citing the potential for lower prices and greater accessibility of dental services, a 1980 report by the GAO recommended the removal of state laws inhibiting the use of expanded function dental auxiliaries to fill teeth.

The Defense of Professionalism

The defense of professionalism has been led by the professions themselves. Their attitude toward the public-policy challenges has been one of reluctant acceptance, at best. The professions generally have rejected the idea that their past actions have not been in the public interest.

The rallying cry of the defenders of professionalism is that the quality of services must be maintained. In the battle over PSRO, many physicians expressed a fear that loss of individual autonomy would destroy the profession. The conservative Council of Medical Staffs said the PSRO law "spells the end of the private practice of medicine as we know it today" (MWN, 1974a:40). Another physician wrote in the *New England Journal of Medicine* that the PSRO law "will have a subtle but profound chilling effect on the honest transfer between patient and doctor. . . . Excellence will inevitably suffer" (LeMaitre, 1974:1323). The American Medical Association, after divisive debate, passed different resolutions supporting PSRO, favoring repeal, and favoring alteration of the law by amendment. Another conservative physician group, the Association of American Physicians and Surgeons, filed suit challenging the PSRO law's constitutionality (MWN, 1974a). All this resistance came in spite of the fact that PSROs will be composed only of practicing physicians. In the end, "The PSRO bill reveals the deep scars inflicted by the medical lobby" (Etzioni, 1974:507).

Medicine's response to the proposed relaxation of advertising restrictions on physicians has been similarly defensive, with an argument based on potential abuses in the quality of care. For instance, the former editor of the *New England Journal of Medicine* wrote that "This intrusion must rank as sheer inanity to anyone who believes that superior medical care and the maintenance of some professional attributes go hand in hand. . . . If the FTC has its way, and doctors succumb to hucksterism . . . no one need worry any longer about deprofessionalization. The process will have run its full course" (Ingelfinger, 1976:334–5).

In the same vein, the chairman of the Council of Deans of the Association of American Medical Colleges spoke of fears of a "less committed profession and a deterioration in the services we [physicians] offer the public" (Krevans, 1979:345); the AMA president stated that advertising by a professional "is the very antithesis of professionalism" (Reynolds, 1976:37); and numerous other physicians voiced similar opposition (Geist, 1978; Relman, 1978; Avellone and Moore, 1978).

The response by physicians mirrors earlier statements by the professions of pharmacy, optometry and dentistry against advertising. In 1977 the American Dental Association justified its ethical canons against advertising because the ethical code was "the direct result of the ADA's desire to fulfill its public-service responsibilities with reference to the maintenance of sound, qualitative standards of dental practice" (Stock, 1978:1208). Organized pharmacy's ethical restriction on advertising was based squarely on the philosophy of professionalism, reading that "A pharmacist should not solicit professional practice by means of advertising or by methods inconsistent with his opportunity to advance his professional reputation through service to patients and to society" (APA, 1975:2).

A final example of the reaction of the health professions to public policy challenges is their response to DHEW's proposal for a national certification council to oversee health licensing boards. Despite the very mild threat to the current "division of labor" in health, the established health professions responded negatively. In a strongly-worded reaction to the proposal, one organization of health professions contends that the proposed council would subvert professionalism: "There is a tendency in the Proposal to view health care as a series of individual procedures performed by a number of technicians. The adoption of this idea would be disastrous to the American people. They need health care which is a series of interrelated treatments administered under the direction of . . . a professional" (FAHRB, 1976:5).

Summary
Thus in the health field, as in other occupational sectors of society, there is substantial turmoil over public policy toward the profes-

sions, and health professions are under growing pressure to furnish evidence of their commitment to provide quality service at nonexploitative prices. Benign acceptance of professional autonomy has given way to public-policy attacks on the anticompetitive nature of many of the standards developed by the self-regulating professions. Professionals have vigorously responded to the challenges, with the defense of professionalism resting on the argument that the quality of services will suffer if attacks on professionalism succeed. "Quality" takes on a broad and ill-defined meaning in these controversies; it may refer to the degree of respect for the professional, the degree of communication or humanism in the professional-client relation, the technical sophistication of the service, or the actual outcome of the service.

At this time, it is unclear whether public-policy proposals will survive the political resistance of the professions, and the effect of these proposals, particularly on the quality of professional services, is unknown. Debate on professionalism in the academic disciplines is growing, however, and that debate may help to direct future policy.

2 *Social Science and the Professions*

Among the social science disciplines, there can be found a great deal of support for the philosophy of professionalism. Several perspectives in the social sciences assert that professionalism indeed is in the public interest. In this chapter we discuss the traditional theoretical rationales for professionalism and the growing disenchantment with those rationales resulting from contemporary social science research on the development and consequences of professionalism. Finally, we identify a weakness in social science research that coincides with the argument used in defense of professionalism in the public-policy conflicts.

Public-Interest Perspectives on Professionalism: Sociology
Historically, the major theoretical justification for the professions in the social sciences has come from sociology. Durkheim (1902:5) advocated that specialized occupational groups become the chief organs of control in society, stating that "an occupational activity can be efficaciously regulated only by a group intimate enough with it to know its functioning, feel all its needs, and able to follow all their variations." Durkheim believed that occupational groups could become the moral "glue" of society, and that they could subordinate their particular interests to the general interest.

Sociologists have long asserted the functional importance of the professions to society. In Spencer's evolutionary scheme, after societies achieve the "defense of life, the regulation of life, and the sustenance of life," they turn to the "augmentation of life," and "this function it is which the professions in general subserve" (Spencer, 1896:180). Professions augment our lives by providing an important function—expert, specialized service.

Classical studies of the professions generally adopt this functionalist view of the role of the professions and their organizations. For example, Carr-Saunders (1928) contends that two chief objectives of newly-formed professional associations are to raise the quality of practitioners and to enforce rules of honorable conduct. He concludes that "the growth of professionalism is one of the hopeful features of the time. The approach to problems of social conduct and social policy under the guidance of a professional tradition raises the ethical standard and widens the social outlook." In a similar vein, Merton (1958:53) says that professional associations "furnish the social bonds through which society coheres."

This optimistic, functionalist view of professional groups has been extended by Talcott Parsons (1968), who maintains that the professional complex has become the most important single component in the structure of modern societies. Parsons observes that the professions are expected to preserve important societal values. Professions support these values "in ways that maintain social stability, but they also generate adaptive innovations congruent with both the interests of their members and the essential values of the total collectivity" (Simpson, 1971:260–261). Simpson elaborates the functionalist position, arguing that while the structure of professions rests on autonomy and associationalism, professionals are guided by moral controls along with linkages to the "imperative control structures of society." Professionals are obligated to develop their knowledge and provide services (moral controls) in return for societal approval of professional autonomy (linkage to the imperative control structures). In theory, then, the state legitimates the self-regulation of a work domain by a particular profession in exchange for service in the public interest. Since the profession presumably monopolizes a body of expertise that is utilized according to a service ideal, the public is best protected through such self-regulation.

Most sociological research on professionalism is predicated on the assumption that professions can be differentiated from other occupations on the basis of several attributes. For instance, Moore's (1970) scale of professionalism is based upon six attributes: whether or not the occupation is practiced full-time; degree of commitment to a calling; formalized organization; amount of specialized education; extent of commitment to a service orientation; and autonomy in the exercise of judgment in work performance. By defining professions as possessing these positive attributes, many sociologists (often unconsciously) support a public-interest view of professions. Indeed, if all professions actually do possess these attributes, it is difficult to argue that professionalism should be discouraged.

Other Public-Interest Perspectives: Economics and Political Science
Additional social science support for professionalism is provided
by the economic argument that governmental interventions—of
which the granting of professional autonomy is one—are responses to public demand to redress inequities in the operation of
the free market (Horowitz, 1980). According to this theory, regulatory schemes are justified by market imperfections in the free enterprise system. Two assumptions made here are that imperfect
markets if left alone will operate inefficiently or inequitably, and
that regulation is virtually costless (Posner, 1974:336). The market
for health services is imperfect because consumers do not have the
ability to judge the quality of services they purchase. Thus in the
medical care market it can be argued that "The professional relationship rises from the significant information differential between
physician and patient" (Evans, 1974:162). Because of consumer
ignorance, professional self-regulation may be introduced as a way
to ensure a minimum level of quality. Leland (1979) reasons persuasively that minimum quality standards can be beneficial, even if
set too high, in markets where the seller has a more accurate
perception of the product quality than the buyer. This rationale is
the justification that has been given for licensing in all of the health
professions—self-regulation is necessary in order to maintain a
minimum level of quality among practitioners.

Pluralist theory in political science can also be used in support of
a public-interest model of professionalism. Pluralism asserts the
value of individual political interests being represented by organized groups which in turn compete for power on behalf of their
members. Individuals will mobilize around any issue fundamental
to a potential group's self-interest (Truman, 1962). In this perspective, organized occupations are competing interest groups that contribute to the smooth functioning of a democracy. If a professional
group is able to persuade the state that the special-knowledge
base of the profession requires the granting of self-regulation,
the state may delegate regulatory power to the profession.
When opposition to a particular policy does not materialize,
the pluralist concludes that no one is adversely affected by the
proposed policy. Based on this largely untested assumption, the
demand pattern for the policy is then described as consensual,
while the policy outcome itself is said to be in the public interest

(Hayes, 1978; Salisbury and Heinz, 1970). Finally, professional groups can be viewed politically as private governments which are "buffers between the individual and the state," important in maintaining a healthy democracy (Tuohy, 1976:669).

All of these social science perspectives are consistent with the argument that the political, economic, and social power of the professions results in the protection of the public interest and advances the quality of services to consumers. However, social scientists as well as public policy-makers have become more skeptical of these claims. A growing body of theory, research, and historical experience suggests that professions in fact may do little to promote quality and that the public-interest perspectives overlook the negative, self-interested consequences of professional power.

Sociological Criticisms of the Professions

Sociologists have challenged the traditional image of professions as homogeneous units granted autonomy by society; consequently a more accurate depiction of professions as social movements with internal competition and conflicts has developed (Bucher, 1962; Bucher and Strauss, 1961; Bridgstock, 1976). Discussions of the process of professionalization have pointed out the political nature of maneuvers by professional organizations to obtain autonomy from the "imperative control structures" (Goode, 1960; Wilensky, 1964; Greenwood, 1966). And because professionalization often is initiated by an occupation rather than demanded by society, the motives of the professionalizing occupation are suspect. As a result, researchers have been devoting more attention to the ability of occupations to organize and manipulate the social and political systems to attain professional status. Berlant (1975) adopts this position in a recent study of medicine in the U. S. and Great Britain. The ethical and licensure systems in medicine, he says, are merely part of a political strategy by organized medicine to gain control over a wide terrain and to optimize income. Ritzer (1977:56) labels this new perspective the "power approach," in which power is defined as "the ability of an occupation (really its leaders) to obtain (and retain) a set of rights and privileges (and obligations) from societal groups that otherwise might not grant them." Consistent with the power approach, Klegon (1978) recommends looking at the "concrete occupational strategies, as well as wider social forces and arrangements of power," related to the ability to obtain and maintain professional status. Professionalization is viewed by such theorists (see Larson, 1977) as the process of translating special knowledge into social and economic rewards.

Sociologists thus have become more critical of the extent to which professionals actually uphold societal values in their work. In his important work on the medical professions, Freidson (1970a, 1970b) finds that the system of physician self-regulation cannot provide a "responsible system of care." For example, in the area of financial practices, Freidson (1970a:363) contends that "the profession [of medicine] in the United States has made virtually no effort to insure that its members do not abuse their privileged economic position by seeking more than a 'just price.'" This financial exploitation can be viewed as a betrayal of the service orientation professionals are expected to exhibit—to serve the interests of clients and the community rather than their own interests. Actual measurement of service orientation is difficult, but Walsh and Elling (1968) attempt it and find that professionalization of health workers diminishes their service orientation.

Even further, sociologists have begun to question the traditional notion that professions possess a certain fixed set of attributes. In contrast to the attribute approach, Becker (1970) suggests that the label "profession" is an honorific term sought and achieved by some occupations. There are no necessary characteristics of a profession, and profession is a folk concept rather than a neutral and scientific concept. So-called attributes of professions may only be symbols rather than realities. Roth (1974) points out even more severe problems with the attribute approach in that it neglects the process of professionalization and results in scientific support for established and developing professions even if the professions may not really possess the so-called attributes.

Recent events support the contention that there are no fixed attributes of professions. In 1928, Carr–Saunders (1928:6) wrote that "Some features of codes of professional ethics are common to all professions. A universal rule is that against advertising." Yet in 1976, the profession of law amended its ethical code to allow lawyers to advertise in the Yellow Pages and certain directories; the National Society of Professional Engineers lost two court tests of challenges to its ban on price advertising (Webster, 1976); and numerous challenges to advertising bans in the health professions were discussed in the previous chapter. Although most professions will probably allow advertising in the near future, it is highly unlikely that the concept of professionalism will disappear.

In summary, most contemporary sociological thought challenges the altruistic, public-interest commitment attributed to professionals. If professionalization is mainly a political power struggle for social and economic rewards, the commitment of the professions to serving the public interest is suspect. The criticisms of the traditional, functionalist approach have several lessons for the study of professions. Researchers should examine the history of professionalizing occupations to see what attributes the occupations seek to attain rather than assigning a fixed set of attributes to professions, and researchers should pay more attention to the importance of political power in the professionalization process. Finally, researchers should test the actual empirical existence of professional attributes in order to evaluate the impact of professionalism on society.

In keeping with these findings, the term profession in this book will refer to an occupation whose elevated social status has been recognized by society. Professionalism is a characteristic of individuals or occupations that indicates to what degree they possess the attributes society has defined as professional. These attributes may vary over time, and indeed may vary between occupations. It is necessary to trace the historical development of a profession in order to identify the attributes used to persuade society that the occupation deserves recognition as a profession.

Before turning to other social science research critical of professionalism, it is interesting to note that contemporary attacks on professionalism in sociology have raised the specter of a witch hunt to at least one observer. About American sociology, Halmos (1973:6, 9) writes that "The contemporary climate of opinion is radically and bitterly antiprofessional. . . . Most of the virulent campaigns of accusations against the personal service professions originate and continue to rage in the United States. American sociologists of the professions are averse to dwelling on the less jaundiced impressions which the personal service professions can and do create." But the antiprofessional climate is not merely a sociological one. Economists, policymakers, politicians and consumer groups also contribute to the milieu. Some further and more direct evidence on the degree to which professions may exploit their relationship with society is available from several political and economic studies of professionalism.

Professionalism as Monopoly Power

Economists have developed a theory of the origins of regulation which is based on the traditional assumption of economic theory in general—that people rationally seek to advance their self-interest. Representative of this approach is Stigler (1971), who develops a theory of economic regulation that centers on the ability of an occupation to secure political power. As a rule, he says, occupations acquire, design, and operate the regulatory process primarily for their own benefit. Occupations seek the benefits of regulation through involvement in politics, and their success depends on the resources that can be mobilized to promote their objectives in the legislature and on the extent to which opposition groups contest their claims. Stigler points out that involvement of the voting public in regulatory decisions is limited by low levels of public knowledge and interest in the subject matter of regulatory policy. Largely identified by a pattern of concentrated benefits and well-distributed costs, regulatory politics can be characterized as involving the actions of various groups to promote their self-interests. Empirical results support the notion that state licensure is an acquired rather than an idealistic form of regulation.

Another classic study of the origins of occupational licensing in economics is that of Moore (1961), who like Stigler compares self-interest and public-interest explanations of licensing. Moore concludes that occupations are selected by legislatures for licensing in the public interest, but the resulting regulations may benefit the members of the licensed occupations.

The political positions of the major health professional associations in recent years are the subject of an analysis by Feldstein (1977), who finds that maximizing the incomes of their membership is the overriding goal of professional associations. Because of the close linkages between state professional associations and state licensing boards, by implication much of state licensing policy may reflect that same goal. More recently, White (1979) analyzes the political economics of the licensing of clinical laboratory personnel. Licensing, he says, has been part of a more general struggle between pathologists and nonphysician groups over the control of the labor market in the industry. The motives of all of the actors in the licensing conflicts, except perhaps for government bureaucrats, seem to have been clearly self-interested.

Most of the economic literature on regulation centers on the consequences of professionalism rather than its origins, and virtually all of the consequences have been found to be negative. Concerning the field of health care, professionalism has been blamed for almost every problem facing the health care delivery system today: high health care costs, dehumanization, trained incapacity, professional insularity and narcissism, low productivity (Frech, 1974; Zimmerman, 1974). Kessel (1970) contends that American Medical Association activities have resulted in restrictions on entry and lack of innovation in medical education, and in a study of dental auxiliaries, Lipscomb (1977:35) shows that "existing task delegation regulations in most states . . . significantly contract the productivity potential of dentists."

More general reviews of health occupations licensing policy have appeared in the past decade, and they reach similar conclusions. Works by Cohen and Miike (1974), Cohen (1973a, 1973b), Dolan (1980), Ellwood et al. (1973), Roemer (1971), and Shimberg et al. (1973) are representative of licensing policy research, and all suggest that major changes in the licensing system are necessary. For example, Roemer (1971:34) reviews medical licensing laws and concludes that "the laws designed a century ago to protect the public against incompetent and unethical solo practitioners have become obsolete; in fact, they have become a straitjacket on the delivery of health services in the quantity and quality the public needs and expects to receive." Research on medical self-regulation suggests that quality controls are minimal. A major study of physician licensing board activity by Derbyshire (1974) reveals that only 0.66 percent of the 300,000 physicians in the U.S. were subject to any kind of disciplinary actions taken over a five-year period.

In studies of other occupations not in the field of health, Pfeffer (1974a, 1974b) demonstrates empirically that the more professionalized occupations have incomes more independent of local economic conditions, suggesting that occupational licensing restricts entry and enhances the rate of return earned by occupations. Rayack (1976) intensively studies licensing boards in three states and concludes that most if not all of them should be eliminated because they restrict entry, limit economic opportunity, impair geographic mobility and do little to control quality. Studying a common feature of professionalism, the minimum fee schedule, Arnould and Friedland (1977) find that the schedules have a substantial positive effect on lawyers' prices. Maurizi (1974) inspects pass-fail rates in several licensed occupations over time and concludes that the pass rate often was used to prolong periods of high income that resulted from increases in demand for occupational services.

A final example of research on the consequences of professionalism by economists is a recent study of North Carolina licensing boards (Baughcum, 1976). Agreeing with earlier findings such as those reviewed above, the author states that "It is rare for economists to come to general agreement on any topic. Nevertheless, the review of economic literature . . . is unanimous in arguing that present methods of occupational licensing are inefficient and more costly than they ought to be." In general, then, most economic research seriously questions the degree to which the professions serve the public interest. The economic theory of the origins of regulation views self-regulation as a product governed by the rules of supply and demand, obtained by persons rationally seeking to advance their self-interest. The grant of autonomy to professions then enables them to set prices above competitive levels and enforce self-interested regulations. Economic regulation, says Posner (1974:343), "serves the private interests of politically effective groups."

The Neglected Element in Research on Professionalism: Quality of Services

It is likely that a backlash to the overwhelmingly critical and cynical view of the professions will develop (see Glazier, 1978). Part of the backlash is based on the failure of contemporary research on the professions to deal directly with the basic historical defense of professionalism—that it raises the quality of services. Very few studies have even attempted to address the question, "Does professionalism increase the quality of services?" In part this deficiency results from the fact that the quality consequences of professionalism are not easy to measure. For example, Holen (1965) shows that licensing restricts interstate mobility and raises incomes but remarks that "Whether the motive for restriction of entry by licensure at the state level is to raise standards of practice or to raise practitioners' incomes is difficult to determine." The lack of statistical control for the quality of services is a deficiency of two economic studies in optometry (Benham, 1972; Benham and Benham, 1975) and is the basis of criticism of those studies by the optometric profession. Similarly, Pfeffer (1974a:478) pronounces this problem in the conclusion to his own study of licensing agencies: "Throughout, no assessment of quality was made. . . . Due to the difficulty, if not the impossibility of objectively assessing quality, studies have dealt with only the more measurable economic effects of regulation and licensing." In the past, the lack of research on the quality effects of professionalism probably has aided the professions, which were able to advance with certainty but without proof the argument that professionals provide higher quality service. But in the antiprofessional mood of today, the tide is turning, and professions are being presumed guilty until proved innocent rather than innocent until proved guilty. For example, White (1979: 124) maintains that because licensing of laboratory personnel may increase costs, "In the absence of any evidence that licensure increases the quality of laboratory tests . . . there rise serious questions about the desirability of introducing new licensure laws or even maintaining existing ones for laboratory personnel." Kessel (1970:41) goes so far as to place the blame for the lack of research on quality on the professionals themselves rather than on academic researchers. Another advocate of the guilty-until-proved-innocent approach is Dolan (1978), who argues that the burden of proof regarding stricter requirements for professional licensure is on the proponents of the restrictions. In his own evaluation of a proposal to increase educational requirements for registered nurses, Dolan concludes there is no proved connection between the proposed requirement and the quality of care.

Some research results do suggest that evaluation of quality changes is important. Recent works by Feldman (1979) and Goldman and Grossman (1978) indicate that price difference for physicians' services may reflect differences in the quality of services. Their findings imply that quality adjustments must be made when measuring the price consequences of professionalism; such adjustments have rarely been made in past economic research. This is an important deficiency because the notion of quality control is the most common defense of professionalism offered by the professions.

Research interest in the quality issue is growing, and scattered results are becoming available. Maurizi (1979) reports data on the number of consumer complaints about general contractors in California, and the implication of his findings is that licensing has resulted in lower quality services over the years. In what they describe as "the first broad exploratory empirical investigation of the effect of received quality of service from state licensed occupations," Carroll and Gaston (1977:41) use evidence from several occupations and professions and also conclude that restrictive licensing may lower overall service quality, in part by reducing the supply of practitioners. They admit enormous data problems, however, and propose that future work be done on an occupation-by-occupation basis. In such a study of one profession, dentistry, Holen (1977) finds that state licensing standards in dentistry appear to increase the quality of services by reducing the probability of adverse outcomes for consumers.

Summary

In summary, it is evident that social scientists and analysts of public policy have produced a wealth of evidence in support of a self-interest model of professionalism—professional status is obtained by politically powerful interest groups who justify their claims on the basis of the public interest yet proceed to further their own interests after being granted professional status. Unfortunately, the self-interest research rarely considers possible changes in the quality of services that may benefit the public, and initial evidence on this issue is inconclusive.

Public Policy, Academic Research, and the Profession of Optometry

Until the mid-1970s, professionalism in optometry was a public-policy issue mainly in state legislatures and in the courts (Begun and Lippincott, 1980). In the 1970s, however, the profession of optometry became an important test case in the national movement to deregulate the economic sector, as indicated by congressional interest in eyeglass price advertising restrictions (Percy, 1975) and FTC activities.

In 1977 the Federal Trade Commission completed a staff investigation and public hearings concerning legal and ethical restraints on the advertising of ophthalmic goods and services. More than 30,000 pages of comments and hearings testimony were produced. The investigation was not directed specifically at the profession of optometry, but it was the optometrist who was usually portrayed as the "heavy" in the eyeglass advertising story (Thelan, 1977). The FTC staff report and the report of the presiding officer of the public hearings concluded that advertising by optometrists should be allowed, to encourage price competition and increase the availability of ophthalmic goods and services (U.S. FTC, 1976a, 1976b). A similar position on the issue emerged from hearings before the Senate Monopoly Subcommittee, which received testimony from the FTC (Optometric Weekly, 1977; U.S. Senate, 1977). Subcommittee Chairman Gaylord Nelson stated that legal and ethical restrictions on optometrists "constitute a classic case of governmental and nongovernmental bodies interfering in the free market to destroy competition, placing the consumer in a very vulnerable position" (Thelan, 1977).

Acting unanimously on their staff's recommendations, the Federal Trade Commission promulgated a pro-advertising rule effective July 3, 1978. The rule preempts state laws and private codes of ethics that prohibit or burden the advertising of prescription eyewear or eye examinations; in addition it requires that consumers be provided with a copy of their prescription after an eye examination, making it easier for them to "shop" for eyewear.

The rule was bitterly opposed by the professional optometric community during its development, and the American Optometric Association filed suit against the FTC's promulgation of the rule.

Earlier, the Association had filed an amicus curiae brief in the Supreme Court case involving advertising by lawyers, arguing that services of lawyers (and doctors) are so important that they should not be reduced to mere commercial transactions (Optometric Weekly, 1977).

Publicity from the FTC actions and Monopoly Subcommittee hearings was perceived as an unfair and malicious attack on professional optometry. One trade journal publisher (Topaz, 1977) wrote that "Never in the history of optometry has so lethal a blow been struck; never in the history of optometry has there been as all-encompassing an indictment of every single man and woman practitioner."

Optometry's substantive objection to advertising is the same defense of professionalism discussed in the previous two chapters, revolving around the quality of care. In 1977, the AOA president maintained that "our primary concern is that advertising will result in a deterioration of the quality of the services and materials provided by a significant number of individuals and companies . . ." (Fair, 1977:9); this concern was also advanced by numerous other leaders in professional optometry (U.S. FTC, 1976b:88; Bennett, 1976; Ancone, 1976). In its 1976–77 Annual Report, the AOA states "In defense of quality health care optometry participated actively in hearings across the land. . . . The vital, but elusive, ingredient of quality in health care has been a major aspect of the AOA's position, while the FTC and Senate Subcommittee have been primarily concerned with price tags."

But the lack of data about quality may work to the disadvantage of the profession. After reviewing several small studies that at least peripherally relate to the quality of optometric services, the FTC presiding officer judged that "There is no evidence in this record which establishes that a continuation of the bans on advertising by either optometrists or opticians would enhance the quality of goods and services furnished to consumers" (U.S. FTC, 1976b:109); the judgment was used in support of the decision to lift advertising bans. Implicitly, the onus for showing a relationship between advertising restrictions and quality was placed on advocates of the restrictions. Challenges to professionalism in optometry will not abate with the recent advertising rule decision. The FTC is undertaking a broader investigation of restrictions on commercial practice in optometry, including restrictions on branch offices, mercantile locations, corporate employment, and use of trade names. The investigation includes original research of the quality of care given by "professional" and "nonprofessional" optometrists. That research will furnish useful information on the impact of professionalism on quality.

Academic Research on Optometry

Two major economic studies have dealt with the optometric profession and in fact are responsible for broaching much of the 1970s public-policy controversies over professionalism in optometry. Benham (1972) utilized a consumer survey and rough estimates of eyeglass price advertising restrictions to find that in states with more restrictive regulations, eyeglass prices are higher by 25 percent to 100 percent. Benham (1972:351) wrote that "Established optometrists and other professionals within a state are likely to benefit if advertising is prohibited, not a surprising conclusion given the enthusiasm with which they support these restrictions." In early 1975, this research was summarized in a popular Sunday newspaper supplement, *Parade*. One month previously, FTC Chairman Louis Engman quoted the Benham findings in a speech urging a closer look at state licensing regulations (RxO, 1975:26).

In more recent work, Benham and Benham (1975) discover that advertising restrictions on eyeglasses are related to lower utilization as well as higher costs of eyeglass services; accordingly, the accessibility and cost of optometric care appear to be sacrificed for the economic self-interest of practitioners. In addition, Benham and Benham contend that professional organization and professional control are important factors in differential eyeglass costs.

The research by the Benhams has been a mainstay in the case against price advertising restrictions on eyewear presented to the FTC, the Senate Subcommittee on Monopoly, the courts, and several state legislature committees (AOA News, 1975b). Recognizing this, the American Optometric Association funded in-house and external critiques of the Benhams' work that are more detailed than will be presented here (AOA News, 1975a; Southern Research Institute, 1976). First, the basic contention in L. Benham's 1972 study, that significant price differentials exist between states, has been challenged. In part, this challenge is based on the fact that his price data came from consumer responses to questions that do not distinguish degrees of quality of service provided.

A second notable feature of the Benham studies is that the proportions of variance explained in the dependent variables are fairly small. In the 1972 study, only 5 percent of the variance in the dependent variable, eyeglass cost, is explained. In the 1975 research, the proportion of variance in the cost of eyeglasses explained by several factors varies in three models from 0.09 to 0.12. Apparently, there are many factors not measured in the Benham studies that influence the utilization and cost of eyeglass services.

The most important unmeasured factor in the Benham studies is the one missing from most economic research and most public policy studies of the health professions—quality. Benham and Benham (1975:446) recognize this limitation of their study, stating that "It must be emphasized that this study has not measured the absolute effects of professional control; it has only examined the differences between highly restrictive and somewhat less restrictive state markets." The effect of professional control on quality is the absolute effect most crucial to a more comprehensive evaluation of professionalism.

The quality issue is a very important one, both for health care providers and the public. In *The Optometric Profession*, Hirsch and Wick (1968:202) forcefully advance their profession's view of the significance of quality care: "This relationship between professionalization and quality of service is a very important one for professional optometrists to understand. It is the real justification for professionalization. Professions require education, governmental control and recognition, codes of conduct, and professional associations for only one reason: *it is in this way that the public may receive the highest quality of service.* . . . The fact remains that total professionalization yields the highest quality of service to the public." [italics in original] Following this line of reasoning, optometrists argue that price differentials between more professional and less professional practitioners will reflect differences in the quality of care. Hirsch and Wick (1968:281–2) spell out this argument in the following passage: "Many Americans go to commercial optometric practitioners believing that they cannot afford the fees of the professional optometrist. These people . . . usually receive an inferior form of optometric service. Far less time is spent with the patient in commercial practices; materials of less than top quality are often used; emphasis is placed on the sale of a pair of spectacles at a bargain price rather than on the total communicative experience . . ."

As is the case with most health professions, there is no academic research showing that professionalism in optometry actually results in higher quality care. Optometrists are unable to cite empirical research that would refute the Benhams' findings, and they have responded instead with both puzzlement and distrust. The AOA *News* published a statistical critique of the first Benham study (AOA News, 1975a). Criticism of the Benhams' research by practitioners has centered on the omission of the quality issue—optometrists argue that higher quality optometric care is the cause of higher prices (Pace, 1975). Not surprisingly, very similar reactions can be observed on the part of the American Pharmaceutical Association and individual pharmacists to the FTC rule on drug price advertising which had been proposed earlier (APA, 1975).

The Research Plan

The research findings of the Benhams call for and enhance the opportunity for closer study of professional development in optometry and its costs and benefits. Given the frequent and strongly worded argument that professionalism enhances quality, it may be too simple to conclude that professionalism serves only to protect the economic and professional interests of selected groups and is ineffectual in protecting the health and safety of the consumer. Further investigation is called for, particularly on the perceived and actual benefits of professionalism.

There are other factors that make optometry a fruitful subject for further research. The profession has attracted little academic attention to date. Several years ago Wardell (1963:222) noted that there had been little sociological research on optometry, and this situation has changed very little since then. The only extensive histories of the profession were written by optometrists themselves (Gregg, 1965, 1972; Hofstetter, 1948; Hirsch and Wick, 1968).

The lack of research on the profession of optometry is surprising. Optometry is a profession in process, not yet having achieved the professional status of dentistry or medicine (see Orzack and Uglum, 1958; Orzack and Janoff, 1976; Akers and Quinney, 1968). As a result, there are substantial interstate differences in occupational restrictions. Control over price advertising in individual states, for instance, varies from no restriction to complete restriction. Professional organization of optometrists is also highly variable among the states; the percentage of practitioners who belong to the American Optometric Association was reported in a recent study to vary from 43 percent to 93 percent (Benham and Benham, 1975). This wide variation, which makes cross-sectional data very informative, is not present to the same extent in such professions as medicine and dentistry.

The relative speed and success of optometry's transition from an occupation to a profession also make it interesting to study, as optometry may represent a model for other aspiring occupations. The nature of the professionalization process in optometry and its empirical consequences are explored in the remainder of this book.

The three occupations that deliver vision care are ophthalmology, optometry, and opticianry. Ophthalmologists (also known as oculists) are physicians (M.D.'s) who specialize in the diagnosis and treatment of eye diseases and other abnormal conditions. They may prescribe drugs, lenses, or perform surgery. Optometrists (O.D.'s) perform eye examinations and prescribe lenses, other optical aids, or visual training when appropriate. Recently they have been allowed to prescribe drugs in some states, but they may not perform surgery. Optometrists refer cases of eye diseases to ophthalmologists. Opticians fill lens prescriptions from optometrists and ophthalmologists; they may not examine eyes or prescribe treatment. It is estimated that consumers spent over 4 billion dollars in 1975 for vision care services, of which 1.75 billion dollars went to optometrists (Trapnell, 1976). In 1974 active optometrists outnumbered ophthalmologists by some 19,400 to 10,700, while there are about 11,000 opticians in the U.S. (U.S. DHEW, 1976a).

Today the prestige and economic success of optometrists approaches that associated with the medical and dental professions (Challenor, 1978; OJRO, 1976). This situation is remarkable in light of the fact that at the turn of the century optometry was only an idea in the minds of some opticians dissatisfied with their place in the occupational structure.

Beginnings of Optometry in the United States
In ancient times eyesight problems were treated by eye pastes, magic, or rudimentary surgery. The use of spectacles to correct eyesight did not occur until their invention in the late 1200s. Churches, the centers of literary activity at the time, were responsible for much of the early development of optical science.

Much of the first two sections of this chapter is based upon material in Hirsch and Wick (1968) and Hofstetter (1948). Some material in the chapter is derived from informal conversations with optometrists and from approximately twelve hours of tape-recorded and transcribed interviews of officials of four state optometric associations and four state optometric examining boards.

Spectacle-making by churchpersons was soon followed by the formation of guilds of lay spectacle-makers. These spectacle-makers, or opticians, usually did not sell directly to consumers, but rather to haberdashers and novelty salespersons. Physicians did not examine for spectacles nor recommend them for treatment, but continued to treat eye problems medically and surgically.

Between 1700 and 1900, spectacle-makers slowly evolved into spectacle vendors and then into spectacle fitters in Great Britain. In the United States, European-type guilds did not exist, but opticians practiced in a manner similar to their British colleagues. Opticians owned their own shops or worked in jewelry stores. In addition, spectacle peddlers traveled the countryside, and spectacles were fitted and sold by some physicians as a sideline or retirement vocation.

The late 1800s in the United States saw the emergence of refracting opticians who gave eye examinations to customers in order to assist them in the selection of appropriate spectacles. Some refracting opticians began charging separate fees for these eye examinations, a practice strongly opposed by physicians. The medical profession claimed that eye examinations and lens prescriptions were an integral part of medicine, not to be performed by non-physicians. Opticians countered that eye examination by ocular refraction constituted an applied arm of optical science and was expressly nonmedical. The name "optometry" was selected by refracting opticians to identify their field of work.

A series of legislative and court battles to legally define optometry began in New York and spread rapidly after 1900, and all states passed laws defining and regulating optometry in the first quarter of the twentieth century. Besides vigorous opposition from members of the medical profession, optometry had to cope with the resistance of many opticians who did not wish to expand their work domain beyond the dispensing of spectacles.

Soon after the first state association was formed in 1896, the present-day American Optometric Association (AOA) was organized. The Association is an affiliation of state associations, whose members may also belong to county, city or zone societies.

Blueprint for Professionalism

Raising educational standards was recognized as a vital first step in the professionalization process. In 1900 there were numerous private training schools in optometry where spectacle-makers could learn how to examine vision and prescribe lenses. The first university program in optometry was a two-year curriculum at Columbia University in 1910, and in 1915 the first four-year program was established at Ohio State. Seeing a need to eliminate lower quality educational programs, in 1922 the AOA sponsored a conference on optometric education that by 1926 resulted in the disqualification of twenty of the existing thirty schools of optometry (Tiffen, 1976:12). Educational requirements for optometrists increased to three years and eventually to four years by 1936, and today optometry is a six-year professional course, with two years of traditional undergraduate college education required for entrance to a four-year optometry school. Most entering optometry students today actually have four or more years of undergraduate college, and competition for admission is similar to that for medical and dental schools (Shannon, 1975b). At present there are twelve schools that award the Doctor of Optometry (O.D.) degree; five of the schools are university-affiliated and seven are independent.

In a short review of the gradual rise in educational requirements for optometrists, Tiffen (1976) has argued that the purpose was to enhance the status and professionalism of optometrists rather than to keep up with technological developments that would necessitate more education. It indeed is true that the history of optometry in the United States has been characterized by an intense drive from within to purge non-professional elements. Several means of motivating practitioners to professionalize were tried. The establishment of the American Academy of Optometry in 1922 was intended to identify a nucleus of highly professional, exemplary optometrists. Another method was the distribution of self-rating questionnaires containing items such as the following, with responses ranked as more professional (1) to less professional (3):

Principal or Employee
1. own practice
2. employed by optical corporation
3. employed by lay corporation

Equipment
1. strictly modern equipment
2. fairly modern equipment
3. insufficient equipment

Fee Schedule
1. separate charge for examination
2. examination included in material cost
3. free examination

Advertising
1. professional card only
2. legitimate educational
3. unethical and/or price advertising

To furnish education to optometrists who had little formal training or professionalism, an Optometric Extension Program was begun in 1928. The program "taught men how to do a better job and convinced them that a professional atmosphere was the best place to do it" (Gregg, 1965:234). Continuing education as a relicensure requirement was implemented in Iowa in 1938, although most other states did not follow suit until the 1960s and 1970s. The drive for required continuing education is officially encouraged by the AOA (AOA, 1971:9).

The intensive effort to achieve recognition as a profession is reflected in the numerous articles devoted to the subject in the early literature. "Why Optometry Is a Profession," "Is Optometry a Trade or a Profession?" and "A Program for Professional Optometry" are examples (OJRO, 1922; Ketchum, 1939; Sheard, 1939). In the following selection one optometrist (Turville, 1920) lists some practical steps for individual optometrists to become professional:

Continuing to remember the public point of view, how are we to enter the professions? The following method is obvious, necessary and somewhat drastic. Let your shops to tradesmen and occupy a private house in a professional quarter. Instead of exhibiting spectacles behind a plate of glass, hang up a plate of brass. Describe callers as patients instead of customers or clients. Require callers to press a bell-push to gain admittance instead of allowing them to walk right in. Transform shops into waiting rooms in which optical apparatus is not displayed, and "sight-testing rooms" into consulting rooms without glass showcases. Let the diagnosis be the main consideration, glasses only remedies for physical deformities, and charges according to the value placed upon services rendered in correcting errors of refraction. Do all this and enter the professions. Do all this or remain forever a tradesman. There can be no half-way between the two.

Optometrists were also urged to develop a "service orientation," which early leaders clearly identified as a key element of professionalism. They were urged to establish clinics to "demonstrate optometry's acceptance of its obligation to serve the needy" (Corbett, 1940:300; Hazell, 1934, 1938). The image of the true professional was of an individual compensated not by money but by a feeling of service, and this image was important in optometry's fight to purge commercialism. Wickersham (1952) described the distinction between professionals and commercialists in these words: "Probably the most important concept in differentiation between a business and a profession is the aspect of service. In a profession the value of the service to the individual serviced is placed above the remuneration received by the professional person. The professions are dedicated to the service of humanity, while the primary purpose of a business is to make a profit on products desired by the consumer."

This distinction still figures prominently in intraprofessional conflict in optometry. According to one optometric leader interviewed, the basic distinction between commercial and professional optometrists is that commercial practitioners "place a very low priority on the patient's visual welfare compared to the selling of merchandise." Commercialists are motivated by their own private-vested interests rather than the public interest.

Commercial practitioners were often identified as those who advertised extensively or worked on a salaried or commission basis for a business corporation. Corporate employment and advertising were regulated in some of the laws defining optometry in the early 1900s, and many other restrictions on commercialism were passed as amendments to the optometry acts, mainly in the 1930s. The stated rationale for the advertising restrictions was that advertising was correlated with incompetent services and low quality materials. In 1928 the AOA declared that "all advertising of price in connection with furnishing of optometric services and materials is fundamentally fraudulent . . . the method of charlatans, whose only purpose is mercenary, and therefore, a sinister practice, in that the public is deceived, which results in injury to vision and health" (Gregg, 1972:116). Restrictions on advertising and employment by corporations were closely related. One leader in optometry contended "There is one direct way to whip the corporate practice menace in optometry, and that is to make price advertising illegal" (Tiffen, 1976:21).

In an analysis of the political history of state legal restrictions on commercial optometric practice, Begun and Lippincott (1980) conclude that the restrictions were introduced and lobbied for solely by optometry's state professional associations. There is no evidence of a public outcry against the excesses of "commercial" practice (see also Tiffen, 1976).

Optometry adopted a national code of ethics in 1944, about twenty-five years after law and medicine codes were formalized in the United States. The code encouraged a service orientation, continuing education, and practices "in keeping with professional standards." The 1946 Supplements to the Code, and the AOA Rules of Practice, formulated in 1950, elaborated these professional standards. Optometrists were advised to dispense none other than ophthalmic goods and to avoid claiming superiority over colleagues. Several restrictions on office displays were offered, such as "no member shall display any merchandise, ophthalmic material or advertising of any kind in windows or in any room of his office for the purpose of inducing patronage." Advertising was limited to publication of a professional card no greater than two columns by two inches in size. In other publications, the AOA encouraged the adoption of professional fee systems that separated a professional fee for service from material costs (AOA, 1966). Recently, the AOA eliminated some of the more restrictive rules in its code of ethics; instead of not allowing advertising, for instance, the new Rules of Practice simply say that each optometrist should obey relevant state laws.

The legislation of one state, North Carolina, illustrates the degree of restrictiveness often enforced at the state level. Under state board regulations, a North Carolina optometrist can have his/her license revoked for such actions as the following (AOA, 1974):

1. The use of lettering exceeding five inches in height when attached or applied to a building, or more than three inches in height on any sign located on a sidewalk or other approach to a building.

2. Practice in or on the same premises where any materials other than those necessary to render professional services are displayed or are offered for sale to the public.

3. The use of signs, posters, decals or any other type depiction of the eye, eyeglasses, spectacles, or any portion of the human head

on any building, approaches to a building or office space, or on any window or in any reception area of any office.

4. The display of any ophthalmic material of any kind in any approach to a building or office space, in any window in an office or in any reception area of an office or building in view of the general public.

In perhaps the most direct approach to achieving symbolic professionalism, the State Board of Optometry of North Dakota requires that applicants answer nine questions affirmatively before they are allowed to take the licensing examination, including: (1) Do you consider Optometry a profession? (2) Would you sacrifice profit for the benefit of your patient? (AOA, 1974)

Optometrists have pursued all of the goals previously listed as attributes of professionals by Moore (1970): full-time practice, commitment, organization, education, autonomy, and service orientation. Recently, optometrists have felt secure enough in professional status to promote legislation to expand work boundaries by legalizing the use of diagnostic and/or therapeutic drugs in optometric practice. These actions have sparked strong opposition from physicians, so much that some optometrists now regret the boundary expansion movement. Diagnostic drug use by optometrists has been legalized in fifteen states, and both West Virginia and North Carolina also allow therapeutic drug use (AOA, 1979). Optometric officials involved in this conflict are acutely aware of the political nature of this movement and are well advised in state legislative politics. Many state optometric associations employ professional lobbyists and have strong "key contact" systems to influence state legislative decisions regarding optometry (Begun and Feldman, 1979; Begun and Lippincott, 1980).

Optometry Today: Measures of Structural Professionalism

In its efforts to professionalize, optometry obviously has accomplished much in a short time. Table 4.1 shows the positions of each state on five indicators of professionalism achieved at the state level in 1975–76, to be referred to as "structural professionalism." Four of the indicators distinguish types of state-level legislation; the fifth shows the percentage of optometrists belonging to the state AOA-affiliated optometric association. Many of the state laws, particularly those governing price advertising, have changed since 1976. This period was selected however because it corresponds closely to the time when price and quality data were collected. Using a summated zero-one scoring system for the absence-presence of each item, states are grouped by their total score, tallied from the four indicators of state legislation. This tallied score will be referred to as "legislated professionalism" and will be used in later analyses. A brief rationale for each measure of structural professionalism follows.

Continuing Education

The first measure of professionalism in the state is whether or not continuing education is required for relicensure (IABEO, 1975:103–4). Optometry has encouraged continuing education as a state licensing requirement both to improve the quality of practitioners and to justify its status as a profession. Strong support for required continuing education has come from the AOA, the national organization of state licensing boards, state professional associations, and state licensing boards (e.g., IABEO, 1974:10,37,64; 1975:58,64; 1976:55,58,103). Developed mainly in the 1960s and 1970s, the profession is proud of its extensive system of continuing education requirements for relicensure. It has proved a useful device for promoting boundary expansion into diagnostic and therapeutic drug use since appropriate training can be easily provided through continuing education.

Optometrist and Optician Advertising

The next two measures of professionalism indicate if price advertising by optometrists and opticians was prohibited by state law or board regulation in 1976 (U.S. FTC, 1976a:34; 1976b:127–9; AOA, 1974, 1976a).

As stated earlier, price advertising of ophthalmic materials (and optometric services) has been viewed as a vestige of commercialism that exploits ignorant consumers (see also Shannon, 1975a; Haffner, 1976; Bennett, 1976). Most practicing optometrists in 1976 opposed price advertising (Aron, 1976), and even in the few states in which price advertising by optometrists is legal, very little actually takes place.

Price advertising by opticians has been opposed by optometrists for several reasons. In many states price advertising is governed by "all persons" designations in optometry statutes, thereby prohibiting opticians from advertising (e.g., Illinois, Kentucky, Maine,

Table 4.1 Structural professionalism measures by state

	Continuing Education Required	O.D. Price Advertising Prohibited	Mercantile Location Restricted	Optician Price Advertising Prohibited	% of State Association Membership[a]
Legislated professionalism = 4					
Alaska	+	+	+	+	100
Arkansas	+	+	+	+	86
California	+	+	+	+	65
Hawaii	+	+	+	+	82
Indiana	+	+	+	+	76
Kentucky	+	+	+	+	85
Maine	+	+	+	+	95
Montana	+	+	+	+	86
Nevada	+	+	+	+	100
New Jersey	+	+	+	+	71
North Carolina	+	+	+	+	95
North Dakota	+	+	+	+	91
Oklahoma	+	+	+	+	96
South Carolina	+	+	+	+	97
Tennessee	+	+	+	+	82
Wyoming	+	+	+	+	80
Legislated professionalism = 3					
Connecticut	+	+	+	−	77
Delaware	+	+	+	−	94
Florida	+	+	+	−	99
Georgia	+	+	+	−	79
Idaho	+	+	+	−	85
Illinois	+	+	−	+	48
Kansas	+	+	+	−	82
Louisiana	+	+	−	+	68
Mississippi	+	+	+	−	75
New Hampshire	+	+	+	−	81
New Mexico	+	+	−	+	100
Oregon	+	+	−	+	65
Pennsylvania	−	+	+	+	61
Rhode Island	−	+	+	+	75
South Dakota	+	+	+	−	72
Texas	+	+	+	−	58
Wisconsin	+	+	−	+	77

Table 4.1 (continued)

	Continuing Education Required	O.D. Price Advertising Prohibited	Mercantile Location Restricted	Optician Price Advertising Prohibited	% of State Association Membership[a]
Legislated Professionalism = 2					
Colorado	+	−	+	−	75
Massachusetts	+	−	+	−	70
Michigan	+	+	−	−	60
Minnesota	+	+	−	−	66
Missouri	+	+	−	−	60
Nebraska	+	+	−	−	71
New York	−	+	−	+	45
Ohio	+	−	+	−	72
Washington	+	−	−	+	100
West Virginia	+	−	+	−	84
Legislated professionalism = 1					
Alabama	+	−	−	−	76
Iowa	+	−	−	−	86
Maryland	+	−	−	−	78
Vermont	−	+	−	−	94
Virginia	+	−	−	−	100
Legislated professionalism = 0					
Arizona	−	−	−	−	81
D.C.	−	−	−	−	63
Utah	−	−	−	−	74

Note: + yes; − no.
[a]State association membership percentages are slightly overestimated due to differences in the sources of numerator and denominator data.

Pennsylvania). In one state, South Carolina, optometrists control the licensing of opticians and advertising is banned in the licensing statute. Optometry has argued that price advertising by opticians destroys the continuity and thus the quality of optometric care. Over 90 percent of optometrists offer dispensing services within their own offices (Aron, 1974), so independently practicing opticians are economic competitors. Optometrists who offer dispensing services usually have lenses prepared by optical laboratories, although a small number employ opticians in their offices. They prefer that patients purchase their eyewear from the prescribing optometrist, to facilitate adjustments of lenses and frames after they have been prepared by optical laboratories or opticians. Finally, optometrists feel that their professional image is demeaned by advertising of eyeglass prices by anyone, because as one optometrist stated in an interview "In the public mind we are optometrists-eyeglasses . . . if the optical dispensing business is commercialized, optometry is going to be degraded." For these reasons, optometrists have opposed price advertising by opticians. In a 1976 survey of AOA members, only 4.3 percent were in favor of price advertising by opticians (Aron, 1976:8).

Mercantile Location

Another state law or regulation, restricting the mercantile location or the corporate employment of optometrists, is the last of the four measures of legislated professionalism (U.S. FTC, 1976a:34; AOA, 1974). Leaders in professional optometry set the 1970s as a target date for eliminating commercialism in optometry (Hirsch and Wick, 1968:176), and they have been moderately successful. Several strongholds of commercial optometry persist, however, in the form of optmetrists associated via employment or lease agreements with business corporations. In several states professional optometry has been unable to overcome political opposition from business corporations (and from the medical profession) to measures that would increase professionalism in optometry (Begun and Lippincott, 1980). In Texas, for example, the legal counsel for the professional association wrote in 1978 that "Commercial segments of optometry, represented primarily by Lee Optical and Texas State Optical, have been . . . contesting the validity and constitutionality of board rules, board statutes, and board enforcement. . . . The lawsuits show a consistent history of commercial optometry's attempts to stymie board enforcement of the optometry laws" (Niemann, 1978:22). Despite the pockets of resistance to professionalism, 1973 data reveal only 2.2 percent of optometrists to be employed by for-profit firms, such as department stores or retail optical outlets (OMRP, 1976).

Professional Organization
The final item in table 4.1 is a measure of the organizational success of professional optometry in each state (AOA, 1976b; Professional Press, 1976).[1] The AOA is strong nationally, with membership by about 75 percent of optometrists. The percentage of practitioners belonging to the AOA-affiliated state associations varies substantially, from 45 percent in New York to 100 percent in five states. Several states, such as New York, California, Georgia, and Texas, also have state associations that are not affiliated with the AOA.

The four restrictions combined into the legislated professionalism score intercorrelate well, as shown by table 4.2. They represent two major thrusts of the professionalism movement reviewed above—to eliminate "commercialism" and to encourage more advanced education. Taken together, the restrictions approximate a Guttman scale, with a coefficient of reproducibility of 0.86 and a coefficient of scalability of 0.56. Eighty-six percent of states possess continuing education requirements, 76 percent optometrist price advertising prohibitions, 63 percent optometrist employment restrictions, and 49 percent optician price advertising prohibitions.

Table 4.2 Yule's Q correlation coefficients for components of legislated professionalism (N = 51)

	(A)	(B)	(C)	(D)
(A) Continuing education required	1.00	.49	.69	.14
(B) O.D. price advertising prohibited		1.00	.67	.89
(C) Mercantile location restricted			1.00	.38
(D) Optician price advertising prohibited				1.00
Total Score[a]	.35	.69	.47	.41

[a]Part–whole correlation coefficients of the biserial type.

The four-item legislated professionalism score has a KR-20 reliability coefficient of 0.59.[2]

Legislated professionalism and state association membership correlate positively but not strongly ($r = 0.23$), suggesting that current membership coverage of the associations does not necessarily reflect past legislative success. Association membership correlates best with optometry's most recent legislative goal, required continuing education ($r = 0.26$), and with employment restrictions ($r = 0.27$). The correlations with optician and optometrist price advertising restrictions, respectively, are negligible ($r = 0.13$, $r = -0.03$). The low correlations indicate that legal restrictions and professional organization may measure different aspects of structural professionalism.

In addition, the legislated professionalism measure certainly has less-than-perfect validity. One factor which probably affects the validity of the legislated professionalism measure is the differing number of years that some of the regulations have been in effect in each state. In North Carolina, for example, restrictive regulations have been in force for many years, and there has never been a significant amount of commercialism in the state. North Carolina is known by optometrists as a "clean," well-organized, unified state. There is little dissension or division among optometrists, and the profession is strong politically and economically.

In contrast, Texas has a legislated professionalism score nearly as high as North Carolina's. The regulations, however, have only been in effect since 1969 (or 1972 in the case of continuing education), so the score does not give a particularly accurate description of the situation. The Texas Optometry Board is split between commercial and professional members, although the professional members dominate and have been successful in attaining restrictive legislation. Several large chains of retail optical outlets employ optometrists in Texas, although the optometrists must be located in offices separate from retail outlets, and two state optometry associations exist in Texas. The Texas Optometric Association (TOA) is the AOA-affiliate, while the Texas Association of Optometrists (TAO) is independent. The TAO was formed in 1972 due to exclusion of a large number of commercial optometrists from TOA membership. Each association sponsors its own continuing education courses. The low AOA affiliated state association membership coverage for Texas (58 percent) is indicative of the organizational situation, but the legislated professionalism measure probably is misleading in this case.

Measuring structural professionalism at one point in time, then, may inaccurately reflect professional restrictiveness from earlier time periods. Since the price and quality of optometric services do not instantaneously adjust to changes in "structural professionalism" we can expect weaker associations than truly exist between professionalism, price and quality. Another potential source of measurement error is that enforcement of the restrictions may vary across states. In general, however, these restrictions are very important to the profession and are enforced stringently once they are in place.

Professionalism in Optometry and the Public Interest

Optometry is proceeding through the traditional stages of professionalization and has sought most of the traditionally ascribed attributes of professionalism. Of major significance in the process have been the extension of educational requirements for licensure and the quashing of commercial practice. The development of optometry clearly illustrates the relevance of viewing professions as heterogeneous or segmented groups with internal conflicts. The role of political power in the internal conflicts has been a major one. Professional optometry has used state government as an important tool in the professionalism movement, and professional associations have been very active as interest groups in state politics.

This scenario, however, does not demonstrate that optometric professionalism is not in the public interest. Obviously, the professionalization movement has furthered the social status of optometry as a profession, but optometrists consistently have proclaimed a public-interest basis for their professionalization. Their literature and leaders all fervently argue that optometry was created to satisfy a public need and that professionalism is necessary to ensure high quality vision care in the United States. In context with the literature, this argument is overstated only slightly in one leader's affirmation that "It is optometry's heritage to stand erect, proud, and unafraid, to enjoy the benefits of its creation, and to face the world boldly and say, 'this I have done for mankind'" (Gregg, 1972:300).

However, as we have seen, virtually all professions attempt to explain and justify their existence in public-interest terms, focusing on the need to upgrade or uphold standards of quality. Little attention is given to other elements of the public interest, such as the price and accessibility of services. To evaluate the rhetorical justification of professionalism, it is necessary to examine empirical evidence relating to the effect of professionalism on the price, quality, and accessibility of services.

5 A National Survey of Optometrists

To gather information on the price and quality of optometric services, a national mail survey of practicing optometrists was conducted between November 13, 1976, and February 3, 1977. A 10 percent sample was selected systematically from a directory of all optometrists in the United States (Professional Press, 1976). The directory is stratified by state and by community, and optometrists are listed alphabetically within communities. After eliminating multiple listings and optometrists denoted as "retired," the sampling frame comprised 22,428 individuals. A total of 2,238 questionnaires were sent. In Table 5.1 the universe, sample size, and number of returned questionnaires are enumerated for each state.

It was anticipated that substantial resistance to completing the questionnaire would be encountered; optometric organizations have been known to encourage nonresponse to some surveys (AOA, 1976d). Optometrists are particularly sensitive about questions relating to price and income because of the FTC price advertising investigation, so responses to price and income questions were precoded into categories.

A neutral optometric organization was sought to provide a cover letter for the survey. The American Optometric Association was not considered because a substantial minority of optometrists do not belong. The International Association of Boards of Examiners in Optometry (IAB), an organization composed of representatives from all state optometric licensing boards, was interested in the study from its beginning and agreed to provide the initial cover letter. In addition, the American Optometric Association and most major state optometric associations and licensing boards were informed of the study, and their cooperation was solicited. The organizations all responded favorably.

The listing of optometrists from which the sample was selected contained several incorrect addresses. Despite the fact that addresses for approximately 60 percent of the sample were verified with an AOA membership roster (AOA, 1976c), of the 2,238 questionnaires sent out, 84 were "returned to sender." In addition, questionnaires returned but not completed indicated that 28 optometrists were deceased, 80 were retired, and 35 were in

Table 5.1 National survey of the optometric profession, universe, sample size, and response by state

	Universe[a]	Sample Size	Usable Questionnaires Returned
Alabama	210	21	8
Alaska	23	3	3
Arizona	187	18	13
Arkansas	208	21	16
California	3,059	305	152
Colorado	252	25	13
Connecticut	306	31	18
Delaware	47	4	2
D. C.	68	7	1
Florida	736	74	54
Georgia	316	31	20
Hawaii	88	9	5
Idaho	102	10	8
Illinois	1,900	190	69
Indiana	645	64	31
Iowa	347	35	21
Kansas	280	28	19
Kentucky	247	24	13
Louisiana	247	25	16
Maine	149	15	8
Maryland	235	24	9
Massachusetts	908	90	43
Michigan	912	91	42
Minnesota	398	39	25
Mississippi	137	14	10
Missouri	487	49	26
Montana	111	11	9
Nebraska	175	17	15
Nevada	55	6	1
New Hampshire	90	9	6
New Jersey	737	73	42
New Mexico	88	9	8
New York	1,923	192	79
North Carolina	384	38	20
North Dakota	76	8	6
Ohio	1,073	107	69
Oklahoma	316	32	19
Oregon	337	34	24
Pennsylvania	1,420	141	61
Rhode Island	141	14	6
South Carolina	200	20	13

Table 5.1 (continued)

	Universe[a]	Sample Size	Usable Questionnaires Returned
South Dakota	93	9	4
Tennessee	382	39	22
Texas	921	91	57
Utah	93	9	6
Vermont	48	5	2
Virginia	271	27	22
Washington	315	31	16
West Virginia	151	15	10
Wisconsin	489	49	31
Wyoming	45	5	2
Total	22,428	2,238	1,195

[a]Hand count of names listed in Professional Press, 1976. Optometrists listed more than once were counted only in the first location. Optometrists marked "Retired" were not counted.

nonpatient care activity. Several more questionnaire recipients probably were not actively practicing optometry; their number is impossible to determine because all questionnaires were not returned.

Two mailings of the questionnaire with a cover letter were conducted, followed by a third mailing of a reminder and a return postcard to be used if the respondent needed another copy of the questionnaire. Questionnaires from respondents who worked less than ten hours per week in optometric patient care were excluded, as were questionnaires with substantial numbers of incomplete items. After the three mailings, 1,195 usable responses were obtained for a 53.4 percent response rate from the original sample or 59.4 percent excluding the known deceased, retired, nonpatient care and "returned to sender" cases.

The response rate was not unexpected. Haffner (1971) obtained a 56.3 percent usable response rate in three mailings of a survey of 4,268 American Optometric Association members. His questionnaire was six pages in length (compared to eleven pages in the present one), and the research was conducted by a well-known organization of optometrists, the Optometric Center of New York, rather than a nonoptometric researcher. Another survey of AOA members, sponsored by the AOA in 1974, yielded a 41.4 percent response, apparently with one mailing (Aron, 1974).

Nonresponse Bias

Respondents and nonrespondents to the survey were compared on three variables—membership in the American Optometric Association (AOA, 1976c), and population and percent urban of county of residency (U.S. Bureau of the Census, 1973). Reponse was significantly (chi-square test, $P < 0.01$) better from optometrists in less populous and less urban counties, and who were AOA members. For optometrists in counties 50 percent urban or less, the response rate was 65 percent; for counties 51–80 percent urban, 66 percent responded; and for counties over 80 percent urban, 55 percent responded. A similar distribution existed for three categories of population size.

Sixty-nine percent of AOA members responded, compared to 43 percent of nonmembers. Some of the difference is due to the fact that addresses of most AOA members were updated, while the addresses of nonmembers were approximately one to six years old. The AOA had 15,529 members in 1976, or 69 percent of the sample universe of 22,428. The AOA claims a membership coverage of about 80 percent of practicing optometrists (AOA, 1976b), and of the survey respondents 80 percent reported that they belonged to the AOA. If those figures are correct, about 3,000 of the 22,428 optometrists in the sampling frame are not in practice. This is not inconceivable, but it is probably safer to conclude that the respondents do slightly overrepresent AOA members.

To evaluate better the representativeness of the sample survey, respondents to the national survey were compared with all active optometrists in 1973 on the following variables: sex, race, age, school of graduation, principal form of employment and geographic region. The comparisons are shown in appendix A. Respondents are somewhat younger than the total active optometrist population, but of the same sex and race characteristics (overwhelmingly white and male).

A large difference is present in the school of graduation comparison. Only 14.6 percent of the respondents attended Northern Illinois College of Optometry, which compares to 21.2 percent of the 1973 national total. Part of the divergence is explained by the attrition of Northern Illinois graduates from the optometric work force since 1973, because Northern Illinois merged with Chicago to become the Illinois College of Optometry in 1955. Survey respondents were more likely than the 1973 national supply to have graduated from the Illinois College of Optometry. Also, the response rate from Illinois was poor (36.3 percent), due to a low quality sampling frame and failure to inform the state optometric association about the survey in advance. Another difference in the school of graduation table is a slight overrepresentation of Southern College of Optometry graduates in the survey, probably due to a slightly higher response rate from the South.

The sample appears to contain an overrepresentation of optometrists self-employed in partnerships or groups (28.0 percent vs 19.7 percent in the national data). Part of the difference is due to the possibility that many cases which would be identified as "other" for the national population are included as "self-employed" in this survey. In the final comparison, there are some small geographic region differences between the survey respondents and the 1973 national population of optometrists, but none of substantial magnitude.

To summarize, respondents appear to be slightly different from the national population of optometrists in that they are more likely to belong to the AOA and to be from smaller, more rural counties. Small differences in sex, age, race, geographic location, school of graduation and form of employment exist but do not suggest any serious bias that will influence later analyses.

Questionnaire Content

Appendix B contains the survey instrument, an eleven-page questionnaire that was developed after consultation with about twenty-five optometrists and a pretest on five randomly selected optometrists in each of six states.

The first section of the questionnaire solicits opinions about various issues in the professional development of optometry. Six questions in this first section were adapted from Hall's Professionalism Scale (Hall, 1968; Snizek, 1972) and are intended to be measures of attitudinal professionalism. A second section is devoted to journal subscription, continuing education, and organizational involvement, all behavioral indicators of professionalism. Information on personal background and patient characteristics is then requested. Finally, a series of questions seek information on practice characteristics. This includes questions on the prices of materials and services, and three possible indicators of practice quality.

Response Reliability

Internal consistency checks were made by computer for responses to many items in the questionnaire. For example, responses to the type of employment question were checked for consistency with responses to gross income and overhead, which were "not applicable" for employees. Number of vision analyses per week and number of referrals per week were required to be less than number of patients per week. Contingent questions were also checked for accuracy of response. Small numbers of corrections were required in the coding of several of these questions.

Secondary data were available only for one variable, AOA membership. Of all optometrists coded from a secondary source (AOA, 1976c) as being AOA members, 99.2 percent (N = 865) reported AOA membership on their questionnaire. An additional 94 optometrists reported AOA membership on the questionnaire but were not coded from the secondary source as members. This is not surprising due to the source date difference of approximately six months and the imperfect reliability of the checking procedure (that is, searching for each survey respondent manually in a huge alphabetized computer printout of AOA members).

The AOA membership question, of course, was not nearly as sensitive as the price and income questions. The 1976 mean net income reported by optometrists in the survey was $34,546. This compares very well with the 1975 mean net reported elsewhere for AOA members, $33,319 (AOA News, 1976). Average prices for frames, lenses and optometric examinations were calculated for each state from the questionnaire data and were correlated with 1970 average state eyeglass prices as reported by consumers in the 23 states for which at least ten responses were available from each source (Benham, 1976). Surprisingly, the 1970 eyeglass price averages correlated strongly with examination price ($r = 0.71$) but much less strongly with lens price ($r = 0.32$) and frame price ($r = 0.16$). These correlations suggest the possibility, as has been argued by optometrists, that the prices for eyeglasses reported by consumers often include service charges. If so, the validity of some studies using consumer data on the price of eyeglasses may be questionable.

A final indication of the reliability of the price data is provided by a 1975 survey of optometrists which reported a mean price of $23 for "diagnostic vision analysis." Prices charged to persons aged 45–64 averaged $25, and persons 65 and older were charged an average of $26 (Trapnell, 1976). The present survey data produced a mean price of $24.35 for examination of presbyopes, most of whom are over age 40.

A reliability check was available for two other variables. Survey respondents reported mean overhead expenses of 54 percent of gross income, similar to the 60 percent total for several "expense" items reported in the 1975 AOA survey. The AOA survey also reported the mean number of vision analyses conducted in 1975 as 1,422. The total calculated for respondents here is 1,645. The difference is not particularly surprising because many respondents to this survey are non-AOA members, who typically have much higher volume practices than AOA members. This evidence, although very selective, suggests that responses to questions generally were reliable.

Measurement Design—Behavioral Professionalism

Sociologists have developed behavioral measures of professionalism that usually represent the different "attributes" of professionals. For example, Rootman and Mills (1974) divide behavioral professionalism into two core characteristics—"service orientation" and "theoretical knowledge." They measure higher service orientation by such items as higher overhead costs, lower fees and less advertising, while theoretical knowledge is reflected by length of training, specialization, journal subscription and association membership. Use of fees and overhead costs as measures of service orientation is questionable, but the other measures appear reasonable. Hall (1968) developed a fifty-item scale with both attitudinal and behavioral items for measurement of five dimensions of professionalism. The scale has been frequently used despite strong criticisms of it (Snizek, 1972).

The measures of behavioral professionalism used here are similar to those used traditionally in sociological studies although an attempt was made to derive the items used here from the historical review of professionalization in optometry and from everyday usage of the term by optometrists. Professional behavior refers here to the degree which optometrists follow the norms of professionalism developed by the occupation.[1]

First, it is clear that professional optometrists should belong to and participate in AOA-affiliated state optometric associations. A scale of AOA involvement was constructed using questions on association membership, meeting attendance, and office-holding at the local, state and national levels (questions 22a–c, 23a–c, and 24b–d) and summing values of 0 = no, 1 = yes for responses to each question. The reliability coefficient for the scale is 0.84.

Second, professional optometrists should be expected to receive professional journals. The number of journals received by each respondent was compiled from question 18, which lists the six journals most commonly received by optometrists. The *Journal of the American Optometric Association* was excluded from the count because it is automatically sent to AOA members and the *American Journal of Public Health* was excluded due to its specialized audience.

Because of the emphasis in optometry on continuing education, behavioral professionalism among optometrists should also be reflected in attendance at continuing education courses, so the number of hours of continuing education credit received in 1976 (question 17) is another indicator of professionalism. It is a continuous variable, with a mean of 21.51 and a standard deviation of 14.11.[2]

Dummy variables were set up to distinguish between other professional and nonprofessional behavior, with the value "1" representing professional behavior. The response to question 47 was recorded either 0 = do not always separate service fee, or 1 = do always separate service fee. Regarding use of advertisement, few optometrists reported advertising prices in 1976 (0.5 percent). Several (8.2 percent) did report advertising the availability of their services, however, so advertising of availability (question 51) was included as a measure of behavioral professionalism. This again is a dummy variable, where 0 = did advertise availability in 1976 and 1 = did not advertise availability in 1976. One further obvious measure of behavioral professionalism, based upon form of employment, was not used because of the small percentage of optometrists who reported being employed by profit-making firms (2.5 percent).

Table 5.2 shows the distribution of the respondents on each of the five different measures of behavioral professionalism. The measures intercorrelate only modestly, though in the expected directions, except for one of the two coefficients that are not statistically significant (see table 5.3).

___

Measurement Design—Attitudinal Professionalism
Attitudinal questions in the survey instrument are contained in the first section (questions 1–16). As mentioned earlier six of these questions (3, 7, 8, and 11–13) are modifications of items in Hall's Professionalism Scale.

A factor analysis of the responses to questions 3–14 and 16 revealed only one well-defined dimension of attitudinal professionalism—anticommercialism. The following questions all loaded high on this dimension, which explained 59 percent of the variance in the responses to the attitude questions:

5. Employment of optometrists in commercial establishments should be prohibited. (agree-disagree scale)

9. The public would benefit from the price advertising of *ophthalmic materials* by optometrists. (agree-disagree scale)

10. The public would benefit by the price advertising of *professional services* by optometrists. (agree-disagree scale)

14. If price advertising of ophthalmic materials by optometrists were common, would you advertise? (yes, possibly, no)

A total score for anticommercialism was constructed by summing responses to these four questions, with each question weighted equally, and with values of 1 = agree or neutral, 2 = disagree, and 3 = strongly disagree to the responses to questions 5, 9, 10, and 1 = yes, 2 = possibly, and 3 = no to question-14 responses.

The remaining attitude questions had little variation in response distribution or failed to intercorrelate as expected and are not considered in the analysis. Table 5.4 shows the distribution of responses on the four selected attitude questions and the anticommercialism score, and table 5.5 presents the intercorrelations of the four questions combined in the anticommercialism score. The anticommercialism score has a Cronbach's alpha reliability coefficient of 0.72.

Table 5.2 Distribution of responses on measures of behavioral professionalism

	N	%
Question 18		
Journals received		
0	16	1.3
1	154	12.9
2	347	29.0
3	438	36.7
4	234	19.6
Missing cases	6	0.5
Total	1,195	100.0
Questions 22a–c, 23a–c, 24b–d		
AOA involvement		
0	172	14.4
1	38	3.2
2	34	2.8
3	95	7.9
4	147	12.3
5	194	16.2
6	194	16.2
7	192	16.1
8	95	7.9
9	34	2.8
Total	1,195	99.8
Question 51		
Advertise availability		
Yes	98	8.2
No	1,092	91.4
Missing cases	5	0.4
Total	1,195	100.0
Question 47		
Separate service fee		
Yes, always	660	55.2
No, not always	507	42.4
Missing cases	28	2.4
Total	1,195	100.0

Table 5.3 Pearson correlation coefficients for measures of behavioral professionalism

	(A)	(B)	(C)	(D)	(E)
(A) Journals received	1.00	.20[a]	.23[a]	.07[a]	.06[b]
(B) Continuing education hours		1.00	.31[a]	.08[a]	.10[a]
(C) AOA involvement			1.00	.24[a]	−.03
(D) Advertise availability				1.00	.01
(E) Separate service fee					1.00

Note: N varies from 1,135 to 1,190.
[a]Significant at $P < 0.01$.
[b]Significant at $P < 0.05$.

Measurement Design—Price

Three questions regarding price are included in the questionnaire. Two questions (66 and 67) related to prices for bifocal lenses and for a specific frame. The questions seemed to be inadequately phrased, however, coupled with the fact that optometrists differ in the way in which they classify their material charges. Some optometrists, about 5 percent, made comments on the questionnaire indicating possible misinterpretation of the two questions. In addition, there seemed to be little systematic variation among optometrists in frame and lens prices, perhaps because most reported wholesale costs to them, which do not vary substantially across the country. For these reasons a decision was made not to rely heavily on the material price measures in the following analyses.

Price for optometric services is measured by the charge for an examination of a presbyope, exluding material and material service charges (question 65). Presbyopia is the deterioration in focusing ability usually associated with aging. Respondents seemed to have no trouble answering the question. In table 5.6 the distribution of responses to the examination price question is reported. For the purposes of later analysis price categories were recoded into dollar values of the midpoint of the categories except for "$50.00 or more," which was recoded as "$50.00." This yielded a mean

Table 5.4 Distribution of responses on measures of attitudinal professionalism

	N	%
Question 5		
Employment of optometrists in commercial establishments should be permitted.		
Agree or neutral	204	17.1
Disagree	312	26.1
Strongly disagree	671	56.2
Missing cases	8	0.7
Total	1,195	100.1
Question 9		
The public would benefit by the price advertising of ophthalmic materials by optometrists.		
Agree or neutral	145	12.1
Disagree	395	33.1
Strongly disagree	646	54.1
Missing cases	9	0.8
Total	1,195	100.1
Question 10		
The public would benefit by the price advertising of professional services by optometrists.		
Agree or neutral	129	10.8
Disagree	349	29.2
Strongly disagree	710	59.4
Missing cases	7	0.6
Total	1,195	100.0
Question 14		
If price advertising of ophthalmic materials by optometrists were common, would you advertise?		
Yes	63	5.3
Possibly	311	26.0
No	811	67.9
Missing cases	10	0.8
Total	1,195	100.0

Table 5.4 (continued)

	N	%
Anticommercialism score		
4	12	1.0
5	29	2.4
6	46	3.8
7	66	5.5
8	113	9.5
9	166	13.9
10	175	14.6
11	191	16.0
12	369	30.9
Missing cases	28	2.3
Total	1,195	99.9

Table 5.5 Pearson correlation coefficients for measures of anticommercialism attitude

	(A)	(B)	(C)	(D)
(A) Commercial employment	1.00	.44[a]	.38[a]	.30[a]
(B) Advertise materials		1.00	.66[a]	.27[a]
(C) Advertise services			1.00	.28[a]
(D) Would advertise				1.00
Total score	.74[a]	.82[a]	.79[a]	.59[a]

Note: N varies from 1,167 to 1,183.
[a]Significant at $P < 0.01$.

Table 5.6 Distribution of responses to examination price question

Question 65 Examination price	N	%
$ 5.00 – 9.99	12	1.0
$10.00 – 14.99	81	6.8
$15.00 – 19.99	212	17.7
$20.00 – 24.99	378	31.6
$25.00 – 29.99	283	23.7
$30.00 – 34.99	138	11.5
$35.00 – 39.99	46	3.8
$40.00 – 49.99	25	2.1
$50.00 +	7	0.6
Missing cases[a]	13	1.1
Total	1,195	99.9

[a]No charge, not applicable, or omitted.

examination price of $24.35 with a standard deviation of $7.20. Lens and frame price categories were also recoded into midpoint dollar values for later analysis.

Measurement Design—Quality

Quality is a broad and variously defined term, so it is important to carefully derive and justify specific measures of quality. In the context of health, the meaning of quality service has been debated in a substantial body of literature (e.g., Egdahl and Gertman, 1976; Institute of Medicine, 1976). Generally, measures of quality have been divided into structures or inputs into services, measures of the process of providing services, and measures of the outcome of services provided. Health services researchers are fondest (in theory) of outcome measures, based on the argument that the outcomes of services are the primary object of concern, and structure and process are only means of attaining outcomes. However, Donabedian (1978) persuasively contends that it is the process of care that ultimately is the objective of quality assessment in medical care. If this is the case, quality can be defined as "degree of conformance to, or deviation from, normative behavior," and structures and outcomes are viewed as indirect means of obtaining information about the normativeness of process (Donabedian, 1978:5). This argument depends on the assumption that the process of providing a service is related to its outcome. Similarly, however, outcome measures of quality are valid only to the extent that outcomes are related to processes.

Measures of quality used in this study are measures of the process of providing the major unit of optometric service—the vision examination. Two measures are the length of the examination and its complexity; the third measure is the amount of equipment available in the office for conducting the examination. Office equipment could be considered a structural or input measure of quality, but if the equipment actually is used in each examination, it becomes more of a process measure.

There are other reasons why process measures of quality are used in this study. First, outcome measures of quality often are not available or cannot be collected feasibly on large numbers of cases with limited financial resources for research. The study by Carroll and Gaston (1977), which sought quality measures for over fifty licensed occupations with very limited success, illustrates this dilemma. In the present study, the basic data collection instrument, a questionnaire to optometrists, feasibly permits only the collection of structure and process measures of quality.

A second reason for using process measures in this case is that such measures are used by both consumers and professionals to evaluate the quality of a patient-provider encounter. As Sloan and Lorant (1976:85) state, "In the case of many if not most types of medical treatment, the patient is not likely to gauge the value of an encounter with a physician in terms of a direct measure of output. Rather, various dimensions of inputs provide the basis for his assessment . . ." In a vision examination, for instance, a consumer is likely to judge a 45-minute examination of higher quality than a 15-minute examination, and the length of examination will affect the consumer's judgments about the price he/she is willing to pay. As a result, it is not unusual to find length of visit used as a quality measure in health services research (e.g., Sloan and Lorant, 1976; Enterline et al., 1973).

Professional optometry has long asserted that equipment, examination length, and examination complexity are realistic measures of the quality of the examination. Some states (such as Mississippi, New Jersey, North Dakota, and Rhode Island) have legal requirements for minimum equipment in an optometric office or minimum procedures to be performed in the examination. "Quickie" examinations are the bane of optometric practice (JFOA, 1954), and there is consensus among professional optometrists that longer, more complex examinations are of higher quality than shorter, simpler examinations (Eger, 1975; Haffner, 1977; Niemann, 1978:19).

However, not all optometrists would agree that these three items measure quality of service. In particular, high-volume practitioners assert that it is outcome of service that counts. In the context of this research, it is not necessary that these process measures be associated with outcomes. The fact that the process measures are used by the profession as indicators of quality, and by inference as determinants of price, makes the process measures interesting in themselves. We are adopting the professionals' definition of quality in order to test their assertion that professionalism raises quality.

Equipment and examination complexity scores were constructed by summation of items from questions 62 and 63 which asked about office equipment and examination procedures. For several of the examination procedure and equipment items, over 95 percent of respondents indicated that they performed the procedure or had the item of equipment available. These items are not included in the equipment and examination complexity scores. As a result, equipment scores were computed by summing 0 = no, 1 = yes values for the following responses to "Which of the following equipment is available for use in your primary practice office?": instrument for visual fields, sphygmomanometer, slit lamp, vision skills tester, intraocular pressure instrument, and subnormal lenses (questions 62b, e, f, h–j). Examination scores were computed similarly from responses to "Which of the following procedures are routinely performed in a complete examination/visual analysis for a *presbyope* in your practice?": indirect ophthalmoscopy, evaluation of accommodation, ductions, blood pressure, recording cup/disc ratio, intraocular pressure, visual fields screening, and biomicroscopy (questions 63c, d, f, g, i–l).

Frequency distributions of the equipment items are given in table 5.7 and intercorrelations in table 5.8. Tables 5.9 and 5.10 give the same information for the examinations items. Reliability scores for the equipment and examination scales are 0.59 and 0.53, respectively. The equipment score items show stronger intercorrelations than do the examination procedure items. A subscale of the examination procedure items, consisting of the four items with high intercorrelations (recording cup/disc ratio, visual fields screening, biomicroscopy and blood pressure), was also used in

Table 5.7 Distribution of responses to equipment question and equipment score

Equipment	Number of Optometrists with Equipment (N = 1,195)	Percentage of Optometrists with Equipment
Intraocular pressure instrument	1,134	94.9
Instrument for visual fields	999	83.6
Slit lamp	961	80.4
Vision skills tester	767	64.2
Sphygmomanometer	509	42.6
Subnormal vision lenses	478	40.0
Equipment score		
0	13	1.1
1	61	5.1
2	104	8.7
3	199	16.7
4	299	25.0
5	328	27.4
6	191	16.0
Total	1,195	100.0

Table 5.8 Yule's Q correlation coefficients for equipment items
(N = 1,195)

	(A)	(B)	(C)	(D)	(E)	(F)
(A) Intraocular pressure instrument	1.00	.73	.88	.25	.80	.48
(B) Instrument for visual fields		1.00	.66	.59	.55	.70
(C) Slit lamp			1.00	.50	.54	.44
(D) Vision skills tester				1.00	.37	.48
(E) Sphygmomanometer					1.00	.34
(F) Subnormal lenses						1.00
Total score[a]	.57	.60	.54	.42	.38	.39

[a]Part–whole correlation coefficients of the biserial type.

the following analyses. Results of its use are not reported but are similar to those reported for the larger scale.

In table 5.11 is presented the frequency distribution for the third quality measure, question 64: "What is the approximate length of a complete examination/visual analysis for a *presbyope* in your practice?" In later analyses the response categories are recoded into minutes, using the midpoint value of all categories except "more than 60 minutes" (recoded as "60 minutes"). This recoding produced an average examination length of 33.33 minutes, with standard deviation of 9.95.

The correlations among the three quality measures—equipment and examination scores, and length of examination—and the price of an examination are shown in table 5.12. Price shows a moderately strong correlation with length of examination, examination complexity, and office equipment. The three quality measures intercorrelate at a moderately strong level.

Table 5.9 Distribution of responses on examination procedure items and examination complexity score

	Number of Optometrists Performing Procedure (N = 1,194)	Percentage of Optometrists Performing Procedure
Examination procedure		
Intraocular pressure	1,124	94.1
Evaluation of accommodation	1,120	93.8
Ductions	823	68.9
Recording cup/disc ratio	789	66.1
Biomicroscopy	438	36.7
Visual fields screening	394	33.0
Blood pressure	269	22.5
Indirect ophthalmoscopy	210	17.6
Examination complexity		
0[a]	1	0.1
1	31	2.6
2	103	8.6
3	243	20.3
4	288	24.1
5	254	21.3
6	168	14.1
7	77	6.4
8	29	2.4
Missing cases	1	0.1
Total	1,195	100.0

[a]In later analyses, "0" and "1" cases are combined.

Table 5.10 Yule's Q correlation coefficients for examination complexity items (N = 1,194)

	(A)	(B)	(C)	(D)	(E)	(F)	(G)	(H)
(A) Intraocular pressure	1.00	.27	.17	.63	.82	.38	.83	−.13
(B) Evaluation of accommodation		1.00	.43	.34	.41	.22	.03	.05
(C) Ductions			1.00	.22	.15	.30	.28	.23
(D) Recording cup/disc ratio				1.00	.55	.47	.45	.27
(E) Biomicroscopy					1.00	.63	.50	.29
(F) Visual fields screening						1.00	.38	.17
(G) Blood pressure							1.00	.24
(H) Indirect ophthalmoscopy								1.00
Total score[a]	.35	.23	.23	.42	.49	.43	.38	.20

[a]Part–whole correlation coefficients of the biserial type.

Table 5.11 Distribution of responses to length of examination question

Length of examination	N	%
11–15 minutes	18	1.5
16–20 minutes	82	6.9
21–25 minutes	175	14.6
26–30 minutes	249	20.8
31–35 minutes	189	15.8
36–40 minutes	177	14.8
41–45 minutes	185	15.5
46–50 minutes	68	5.7
51–55 minutes	9	0.8
56–60 minutes	29	2.4
60+ minutes	12	1.0
Missing cases	2	0.2
Total	1,195	100.0

Table 5.12 Pearson correlation coefficients for price and quality measures

	(A)	(B)	(C)	(D)
(A) Examination price	1.00	.36[a]	.39[a]	.41[a]
(B) Examination complexity		1.00	.51[a]	.36[a]
(C) Office equipment			1.00	.28[a]
(D) Examination length				1.00

Note: N varies from 1,181 to 1,194.
[a]Significant at $P < 0.01$.

Professionalism, Price, and Quality in Optometry

Most optometrists would argue that professionalism improves the quality of optometric services and that the prices charged reflect only this improved quality. Critics, however, would argue that professional monopoly leads to an increase in prices that is independent of, or disproportionate to, the increases in quality.

A conceptual model underlies much of this presentation. Both price and quality are conceived as outcome variables explained by professionalism and residual factors. In addition, price is affected by quality. The public-interest perspective would hypothesize that the "causal path" from professionalism to quality is an important and strong one, while the impact of professionalism on price (if it exists) is a result of quality improvements. Self-interest perspective supporters, on the other hand, would predict that the direct causal path from professionalism to price is the strongest relationship in the conceptual model.

Professionalism, Price, and Quality: A Preliminary Look

To obtain an introductory observation of the impact of professionalism on price and quality, mean price and quality measures for optometric examinations are given in tables 6.1 and 6.2 for different levels of professionalism. The professionalism measures are the behavioral, attitudinal, and structural indicators described in the last chapter.

As table 6.1 illustrates, examination prices are substantially higher in states with professional restrictions and among optometrists considered more "professional." In all cases except one the differences are statistically significant at the 0.01 level. Mean examination prices are about 20 percent higher for optometrists who are highly involved in the AOA, do not advertise, have anticommercial attitudes, or report many continuing education hours. Prices similarly are higher by over 20 percent for optometrists in states with high legislated professionalism scores and high AOA membership. The results in table 6.1 are consistent with the notion that professional activity and professional restrictions lead to higher prices for services.

Table 6.1 Mean price of optometric examination by levels of
professionalism

	Examination Price ($)	N
Structural Professionalism		
Legislated professionalism		
Low (0–2)	22.40	415
Medium (3)	23.87	410
High (4)	27.18[a]	357
State AOA membership		
Low (45–60%)	20.85	269
High (61–100%)	25.34[a]	913
Behavioral Professionalism		
Journals received		
Low (0–2)	23.07	513
High (3–4)	25.36[a]	664
Continuing education hours		
Low (0–11)	22.32	240
Medium (12–29)	23.74	613
High (30+)	27.31[a]	297
AOA involvement		
Low (0–4)	21.49	477
High (5–9)	26.29[a]	705
Advertising		
Yes	20.74	98
No	24.70[a]	1,079
Separate service fee		
No	24.01	503
Yes	24.65	652
Attitudinal Professionalism		
Anticommercialism		
Low (3–8)	21.38	262
Medium (9–11)	24.66	527
High (12)	26.14[a]	366

[a]F value for between–groups difference significant at $P < 0.01$.

Table 6.2 Mean quality levels of optometric examination by levels of professionalism

	Examination Length (minutes)	Examination Complexity Score	Office Equipment Score	Minimum N
Structural Professionalism				
Legislated professionalism				
Low (0–2)	31.92	4.26	3.99	418
Medium (3)	33.98	4.33	4.06	412
High (4)	34.23[a]	4.41	4.14	362
State AOA membership				
Low (45–60%)	30.35	3.93	3.55	271
High (61–100%)	34.21[a]	4.45[a]	4.21[a]	921
Behavioral Professionalism				
Journals received				
Low (0–2)	32.16	3.98	3.68	517
High (3–4)	34.27[a]	4.60[a]	4.36[a]	670
Continuing education hours				
Low (0–11)	30.86	3.63	3.36	243
Medium (12–29)	32.76	4.28	4.05	619
High (30+)	36.36[a]	5.04[a]	4.68[a]	299
AOA involvement				
Low (0–4)	30.58	3.80	3.38	484
High (5–9)	35.21[a]	4.69[a]	4.52[a]	708
Advertising				
Yes	28.28	3.87	3.36	98
No	33.80[a]	4.37[a]	4.12[a]	1,090
Separate service fee				
No	33.25	4.10	3.90	505
Yes	33.55	4.51[a]	4.19[a]	660
Attitudinal Professionalism				
Anticommercialism				
Low (3–8)	28.72	3.90	3.60	265
Medium (9–11)	34.02	4.43	4.19	531
High (12)	35.63[a]	4.51[a]	4.19[a]	368

[a] F value for between–groups difference significant at $P < 0.01$.

However, table 6.2 suggests that there may be some justification for the higher prices charged by the more professional optometrists. For optometrists with high AOA involvement, for instance, examination length averages about five minutes more, more procedures are performed, and more equipment is available for use. Similar differences are present for most of the measures of professionalism. In all 24 of the comparisons, mean quality measures are higher for the more professional optometrists; the differences are statistically significant in all but three cases.

In order to take a closer look at how each of the four regulations comprising legislative professionalism affects price and quality, table 6.3 exhibits mean price and quality values for optometrists in states with and without the various restrictions. The most striking illustrations of price and quality differences are produced by the continuing education and mercantile location regulations. In particular, prices are 25 percent higher in states that require continuing education, examinations are substantially more complex, and offices are better equipped. Length of examination shows little variation between more and less regulated states. Optometrists

Table 6.3 Mean price and quality of optometric examination by levels of legislated professionalism

	Examination Price ($)	Examination Length (minutes)	Examination Complexity Score	Office Equipment Score	Minimum N
Continuing education required					
No	20.00	31.01	3.77	3.63	166
Yes	25.06[a]	33.71[a]	4.42[a]	4.13[a]	1,016
O.D. advertising prohibited					
No	23.81	33.17	4.50	4.26	229
Yes	24.48	33.37	4.29	4.01	953
Optician advertising prohibited					
No	23.73	33.03	4.43	4.17	520
Yes	24.84[a]	33.57	4.25	3.97	662
Mercantile location prohibited					
No	22.60	32.39	4.17	3.90	427
Yes	25.34[a]	33.87	4.42[a]	4.15[a]	755

[a] F value for between–groups difference significant at $P < 0.01$.

grouped by state advertising regulations average somewhat higher prices but do not show notably higher quality levels. Nonetheless, quality is higher in the more restrictive environments in all five of the statistically significant quality comparisons, just as price is higher in the three price comparisons with significant differences.

Does Professionalism Raise Price?

In combination the three previous tables suggest that higher professionalism is associated with higher quality and higher price, and both public-interest and self-interest proponents do appear to have a basis for their arguments. Before drawing conclusions, however, it is necessary to examine the relationships taking into account other variables which may explain price and quality differences among optometrists.

To evaluate the impact of professionalism on price independent of differences in quality and a host of other control variables, an ordinary least squares linear regression analysis of price was conducted using the variables listed in table 6.4. (Means and standard deviations of the variables are given in appendix C.)

In order to compute the percentage of the variance in price which is explained by professionalism after accounting for the influence of quality and other factors, the variables were entered in groups. Entered first in the regression were a group of eleven control variables which affect price but are not of particular interest here.

Patient income status (as reported by the optometrist) and county urbanization are characteristics which are expected to affect price. Higher income status of patients should lead to higher prices charged, while county urbanization is a proxy for unmeasured variations in the cost of labor, office space, and other inputs into optometric services. The anticipated direction of the urbanization effect is ambiguous, as some factors, such as office space, may be more expensive in urban areas but others, such as skilled labor, may be cheaper. The urbanization variable may also measure the apparently higher levels of competition among optometrists (and between optometrists and other providers) in urban areas, which can be expected to lower prices (Begun and Lippincott, 1980).

The price charged for a specific lens and frame are introduced into the equation because of the possibility that some optometrists inflate their material charges as an alternative to raising examination prices. This would produce a negative relationship between material and service prices.

Number of examination rooms and overhead are indicative of greater investment in the practice and should act to increase prices. Higher volume, indicated by examinations per week and more hours practiced, should decrease prices due to economies of scale. Based on findings from studies of other types of medical services, a greater percentage of third-party-reimbursed examinations may allow optometrists to charge higher prices. Also, specialist practitioners can be expected to command a premium for their services. Finally, more recent graduates of optometry school may charge more due to their more sophisticated training. On the other hand, their lack of experience may justify lower, rather than higher, prices.

Entered next in the regression were the quality measures discussed earlier—length of examination, office equipment, and examination complexity. Entering the quality items at this point in the regression has the effect of adjusting price for quality before examining the impact of professionalism on price. We hypothesize that higher quality will lead to higher prices.

The measures of professionalism are entered into the analysis last. As we have seen, there are conflicting hypotheses about the effect of professionalism on quality-adjusted price and thus on the expected sign of these coefficients.

The results of the regression analysis are shown in table 6.4. A total of 43 percent of the variance in price is explained by the regression model. Control variables account for almost one-half of the explained variance (19 percent), while quality measures explain 14 percent. The remaining 10 percent of the variance is accounted for by the measures of professionalism. Both quality and professionalism, therefore, do make contributions to explaining price. Because of intercorrelations among the quality and professionalism measures (in one case as high as $r = 0.47$), it is not necessarily true that quality explains more of the variance in price than does professionalism. The higher percentage of variance explained may be due to the fact that quality was entered into the regression equation before professionalism.[1] In any event, the measures of professionalism are positively related to price after accounting for the effects of the control and quality variables.

The reader's attention is directed next to the magnitude and direction of relationships between price and the statistically signif-

Table 6.4 Regression analysis of examination price

	Unstandardized Regression Coefficient	t statistic[a]
Control variables		
Patient income status	.726	2.330
Urbanization	.003	.417
Frame price	.096	2.541
Lens price	.035	2.051
Examination rooms	.442	3.182
Overhead	−.020	−1.676
Examinations per week	−.060	−5.938
Annual patient care hours	−.001	−3.360
Third party income	.060	4.650
Specialty practice	.027	2.451
Year of graduation	.010	.707
Examination quality		
Examination length	.122	6.422
Examination complexity	.304	2.375
Office equipment	.536	3.619
Structural professionalism		
Legislated professionalism	1.314	7.832
State AOA membership	.063	5.464
Behavioral professionalism		
Journals received	.457	2.599
Continuing education hours	.041	3.259
AOA involvement	.402	5.148
No advertising	−.651	−1.071
Separate service fee	.518	1.525
Attitudinal professionalism		
Anticommercialism score	.354	4.404
Constant	−.069	

[a] t statistic of absolute value of 1.65 significant at $P = 0.05$ in one-tailed test, 1.96 in two-tailed test. N = 1,182. Means assigned to missing values of independent variables.
$\bar{R}^2 = 0.43$.

Brief names and descriptions of variables in regression analyses

Price
Examination price: Price of examination of presbyope in dollars (question 65).

Control variables
1. Patient income status: Economic status of patients in three categories, where 1 = under $10,000, 2 = $10,000–$15,000, 3 = over $15,000 (question 42).
2. Urbanization: Percentage of county population living in urban areas (U.S. Bureau of the Census, 1973).
3. Frame price: Charge for specified frame in dollars (question 67).

4. Lens price: Charge for specified bifocal lenses in dollars (question 66).
5. Examination rooms: Number of examining rooms (question 61).
6. Overhead: Percentage of gross income spent on overhead (question 69).
7. Examinations per week: Number of examinations per week (question 58).
8. Annual patient care hours: Hours per year spent in patient care (questions 31a, 32).
9. Third party income: Percentage of income from other third party (question 45).
10. Specialty practice: Percentage of patient care time devoted to specialty practice (questions 34b–d).
11. Year of graduation: Year of graduation from optometry school (question 29).

Examination quality
1. Examination length: Length of examination of presbyope in minutes (question 64).
2. Examination complexity: Score indicating number of eight selected procedures performed in examination of a presbyope (questions 63c, d, f, g, i–l).
3. Office equipment: Score indicating number of six selected equipment items available in office (questions 62b, e, f, h–j).

Structural professionalism
1. Legislated professionalism: Score indicating number of four legal constraints enforcing professionalism present in a state.
2. State AOA membership: Percentage of optometrists in a state who belong to the American Optometric Association-affiliated state association.

Behavioral professionalism
1. Journals received: Number of professional journals received (questions 18b–e).
2. Continuing education hours: Hours of continuing education credit received in 1976 (question 17).
3. AOA involvement: Score indicating number of participations in nine selected types of AOA involvement (questions 22a–c, 23a–c, 24b–d).
4. No advertising: Dummy variable where 0 = did advertise availability in 1976, 1 = did not advertise availability in 1976 (question 51).
5. Separate service fee: Dummy variable where 0 = do not always separate service fee, 1 = always separate service fee (question 47).

Attitudinal professionalism
Anticommercialism score: Anticommercialism attitude scale, ranging from 3 (low anticommercialism) to 12 (high anticommercialism) (questions 5, 9, 10, and 14).

icant explanatory variables. The unstandardized regression coefficient for each independent variable in table 6.4 indicates the expected change in the dependent variable (price) with a change of one unit in the independent variable, holding all other independent variables in the equation constant.

Highly significant among the control variables are the number of examinations per week and annual patient-care hours, both indicative of the volume of practice. An increase in the volume of practice by ten examinations per week is associated with a $0.60 decline in average examination price. Contrary to expectations, higher examination prices are associated with higher frame and lens prices and with lower overhead percentages, the latter perhaps reflecting an effect of "number of years in practice," which was not directly measured. As expected, more examination rooms are associated with higher prices, and third party income percentage has a positive effect on examination prices, with a 10 percent increase in the percentage of income from third parties being associated with a $0.60 increase in examination price. Prices climb as patient income status does, and optometrists who specialize are likely to charge higher examination prices. The effects of urbanization and year of graduation are small and not statistically significant.

The quality measures register highly significant coefficients in the regression, all three showing positive relationships with price. An increase in the length of an examination of ten minutes is associated with an increase of $1.22 in examination price. A change of one more equipment item raises price $0.54, and one more examination procedure raises price $0.30.

After consideration of the effects of the fourteen control and quality variables, professionalism still has a major effect on price. An increase of one unit in the legislated professionalism score changes price by $1.31, and a 10 percent increase in state AOA membership raises price by $0.63. Among the individual-level measures of professionalism, AOA involvement and anticommercialism attitudes prove to be most significantly related to price. Optometrists who receive more journals and more continuing education credits also are likely to charge higher prices, and optometrists who separate service and material fees charge about $0.50 more. The only professionalism measure not positively related to price is "no advertising," and its coefficient is not statistically significant.

Do Licensing Regulations Raise Price?

A topic of current public policy interest, as we have seen, involves the effect of state-level restrictions on the price of health services. To look more closely at these effects, coefficients were computed for a regression model identical to the one in table 6.4 except that items in the legislated professionalism score were separated into four dummy variables. This permitted inspection of the effect of particular state restrictions on individual price differences, controlling for quality.

All coefficients of the state restrictions were positive, indicating that prices are higher in the more restrictive states for each of the regulations. Optometrists in states that require continuing education averaged $2.61 higher in examination price than in states without the requirement. Unstandardized regression coefficients for optician and optometrist price advertising restrictions were 1.60 and 0.74 respectively, and the coefficient for the commercial location and employment restrictions was 1.13. All of the coefficients except the optometry advertising coefficient were statistically significant at the 0.01 level.

It is somewhat surprising that advertising restrictions on opticians, who sell eyewear, seem to affect significantly the prices of examinations charged by optometrists. This possibility, discussed in more detail by Begun and Feldman (1979), may be due to the fact that consumers often purchase eyewear and eye examinations jointly, and average eyewear and eye examination prices in states are highly correlated.

Because of FTC investigations of price advertising restraints on optometrists and opticians, the magnitude of the effects of these restrictions is particularly important. Advertising restraints on opticians and optometrists can be combined to produce one dummy variable indicating whether ophthalmic advertising is totally prohibited or not. Inserting this new variable into the price regression reported earlier yields a coefficient of 1.89, a bit higher than the optician's ban coefficient reported earlier (1.60). In states that do not allow advertising by optometrists and opticians, then, prices are higher by $1.89, ceteris paribus. Relative to the national average price of $24.35, examination prices are 7.8 percent higher in the restrictive states.

Alternative estimates of the effect of advertising restrictions on the mean price for optometric examinations are given in several other sources (Feldman and Begun, 1978, 1980; Begun and Feldman, 1979). Using different specifications of the functional relationship between price and the independent variables, those estimates show that vision examination prices are higher by from 9 percent to 16 percent in states that prohibit advertising by both opticians and optometrists. It is estimated that the 1978 FTC ruling that preempted such bans will lower prices by some 11 percent (Begun and Feldman, 1979:143). In addition, the variance of prices is found to be higher in states that restrict advertising.

Although the exact magnitude of the advertising ban effect is subject to debate, it clearly is present. The estimate shown herein is smaller than those reported in the other studies cited because those studies used more exclusive definitions of advertising restrictions. (That is, more states in this analysis are classified as restrictive. The more exclusively one defines the advertising ban, the stronger its estimated impact is.)

State Prices of Optometric Examinations

Since state governments control the licensing process, there is substantial public policy interest in the statewide impact of licensing regulations. A final method of analysis directed at the influence of professionalism and quality on price will focus on mean examination prices in the thirty-three states that had ten or more survey respondents. The other states are excluded because of the high standard error in many of the means computed on less than ten cases. The method of analysis involves standardizing the mean state examination prices for examination quality and for several other variables shown above to have highly significant effects on price. The variables selected are examination length, examination complexity, office equipment, third party income, annual patient care hours, examinations per week and examination rooms. These are the three quality measures along with the four variables from table 6.4 with the highest t statistic values, exluding all measures of professionalism. The method will compute the mean price in each of the thirty-three states for an examination having average values for all optometrists in the thirty-three states on each of the seven standardizing variables.

For example, North Carolina is a state with a high score on legislated professionalism (4) and high state organization (95 percent of optometrists belong to the state association). The mean price of an examination is $30.38, well above the thirty-three state average of $24.29. North Carolina's values on several of the seven standardizing variables suggest that the higher price might be partially justifiable. For example, the office equipment score for North Carolina optometrists is higher (4.65 compared to 4.05) and examinations average almost two minutes longer than the thirty-three state average. In New York, with a legislated professionalism score of only 2 and low organization (45 percent of optometrists belong to the state association), examination price averages only $18.21. But the New York optometrist's examination length is over five minutes less than the thirty-three state average, office equipment score is 3.24 compared to 4.05, and the score on examination complexity averages 3.47 compared to 4.34. Standardization for these and other characteristics will obviously allow a more accurate comparison of the mean state examination prices.

The standardization method uses the regression equation of the seven standardizing characteristics on examination price, estimated for all cases in the thirty-three states. Substitution of the state averages for each variable in the regression equation yields predicted state prices. It is assumed that predicted state prices differ from the thirty-three state average price by a constant amount. To compute standardized prices for states, predicted state prices are substracted from actual state prices, and the difference is added to the thirty-three state average price. The result, column 2 in table 6.5, is the price of a "thirty-three state average" optometric examination in each state. The technique is outlined in greater detail in Feldman (1979).

Traditionally, this method of adjustment is referred to as "quality adjustment." Since measures of quality here have been confined to characteristics directly affecting an optometric examination, it is more accurate to say that prices are adjusted by the seven major characteristics that influence price, exclusive of professionalism.

Standardization, however, makes only small differences in mean prices and fails to alter the ranking of most of the states on mean price to any great extent. This fact can be observed in table 6.5, which gives unadjusted and standardized mean prices for each of the thirty-three states. A positive amount in column 3 indicates that because of lower quality (and/or other factors) in a state, standardized price is higher than unadjusted price. For example, after standardization New York's average price rises from $18.21 to

Table 6.5 Mean examination price, unadjusted and standardized, for states with ten or more respondents

	Mean Price, Unadjusted	Mean Price, Standardized[a]	Standardized Price Minus Unadjusted Price	N
Arizona	$24.42	$23.02	− $1.40	13
Arkansas	28.28	28.02	− .26	16
California	28.45	27.55	− .90	148
Colorado	27.88	26.00	− 1.88	13
Connecticut	26.25	24.43	− 1.82	18
Florida	28.06	25.71	− 2.35	54
Georgia	25.13	25.74	.61	20
Illinois	21.85	22.72	.87	69
Indiana	24.33	23.95	− .38	30
Iowa	22.02	21.74	− .28	21
Kansas	27.11	26.09	− 1.02	19
Kentucky	20.96	23.31	2.35	13
Louisiana	22.50	22.83	.33	15
Massachusetts	22.85	22.92	.07	43
Michigan	23.45	23.91	.46	42
Minnesota	23.30	23.63	.33	25
Mississippi	24.00	23.45	− .55	10
Missouri	19.80	20.65	.85	25
Nebraska	23.17	23.24	.07	15
New Jersey	25.18	24.43	− .75	42
New York	18.21	21.29	3.08	77
North Carolina	30.38	29.78	− .60	20
Ohio	22.32	22.42	.10	69
Oklahoma	22.50	23.90	1.40	19
Oregon	30.63	27.67	− 2.96	24
Pennsylvania	21.43	21.93	.50	61
South Carolina	27.50	26.85	− .65	13
Tennessee	26.25	25.79	− .46	22
Texas	21.74	23.89	2.15	56
Virginia	24.77	25.04	.27	22
Washington	28.11	26.93	− 1.18	14
West Virginia	27.00	26.93	− .07	10
Wisconsin	22.74	21.48	− 1.26	31

[a]Price in each state of an examination with the following thirty-three state average characteristics: examination length, examination complexity, office equipment, third party income, examinations per week, examination rooms and annual patient care hours. State averages should be used cautiously if at all due to small sample sizes.

$21.29. This is the largest adjustment among the thirty-three states, however, and most adjustments are relatively small. The range of average prices shrinks, but relative positions do not change drastically. This is shown more clearly in table 6.6, which groups optometrists in states by levels of structural professionalism. Price differences between levels of professionalism grow smaller after standardization, but price differences between states which do or do not prohibit price advertising actually grow larger after standardization. In general, it can be concluded that even after standardizing the state mean prices, a definite relationship between price and structural professionalism exists.

The effect of legislated professionalism items on price after quality adjustment in this analysis can be compared to the effects estimated earlier by regression coefficients. The size of the effect of professionalism on price in table 6.6 is reflected by the difference in mean price at the various levels of the legislated professionalism measures. States with continuing education requirements have a standardized mean price $3.03 higher than states not requiring continuing education, for example. This compares to the $2.61 effect demonstrated in the regression model. The effect of optometrist price advertising prohibitions is $0.90 in table 6.6, compared to $0.74 in the earlier regression. The other effects as calculated in table 6.7 differ more from the regression analysis results: the optician price advertising effect is $0.84 compared to $1.60 earlier and the mercantile location restriction effect is $2.08 compared to $1.13. Because a greater number of variables is included in the regression analysis and the standardization analysis is based on gross state averages rather than individual characteristics, the regression results are probably more trustworthy.

Some methodological problems should temper the interpretation of the legislated professionalism effects. As discussed earlier, it is difficult to measure the "true" degree of professional restrictiveness and the price and quality differences between the more regulated and less regulated states are probably attenuated. Nonresponse bias should influence interpretation of the results. The range of prices across states is probably underestimated because the underrepresented high volume, low priced "commercial" optometrists are concentrated in particular states. Analysis of nonresponse bias by Begun (1979) and Feldman and Begun (1978) leads to the conclusion that the effect of the optician ban is overestimated, the effect of the optometrist ban underestimated, and

Table 6.6 Mean examination price for 33 states before and after standardization, by levels of structural professionalism

	Mean Examination Price Before Standardization	Mean Examination Price, Standardized[a]	N
State AOA membership			
Low (45–60%)	$20.82	$22.54	273
High (61–100%)	25.43	24.88	828
Legislated professionalism			
Low (0–2)	22.37	22.94	394
Medium (3)	24.01	23.84	379
High (4)	26.92	26.44	328
Continuing education required			
No	20.02	21.69	153
Yes	24.98	24.72	948
O.D. advertising prohibited			
No	23.89	23.56	207
Yes	24.38	24.46	894
Optician advertising prohibited			
No	23.89	23.82	477
Yes	24.60	24.66	624
Mercantile location restricted			
No	22.47	22.97	399
Yes	25.33	25.05	702

[a]Mean is weighted by number of sample cases in each state in each category.

the overall effect of legislated professionalism is slightly underestimated.

In interpreting the preceding tables, finally, it is important to note that the average state prices reported in table 6.5, indeed all of the reported average price and quality values, are not the values actually faced by consumers. First, optometrists who perform higher quality and higher priced examinations produce fewer examinations per year. Second, this sample of optometrists probably overrepresents AOA members, which raises average price and quality. Average price and quality faced by consumers most likely are lower than the levels reported here.

Does Professionalism Raise Quality?

These analyses of optometric prices suggest that elements of both the public and self-interest perspectives are correct. Professionalism indeed is associated with higher price after controlling for quality, as has been charged by critics of professionalism. Characteristics of professionalism do have an independent and positive impact on price. At the same time, the data suggest that consumers receive a somewhat different service for higher prices—in this case, a longer and more technically advanced service.

The possibility that professionalism increases not only examination price but examination quality can be further evaluated by the regression analyses presented in table 6.7, in which examination length and complexity are explained by several control variables along with the variables measuring professionalism.

Seven control variables are statistically significant at the 0.05 level in explaining examination length. Among the control variables overhead percentage, examination complexity and office equipment are positively associated with examination length, while the number of examinations per week and year of graduation are negatively related. As hypothesized, all eight of the professionalism measures are associated positively with examination length, with continuing education participation, anticommercial attitudes, and legislated professionalism having significant coefficients.

In the examination complexity regression, 36 percent of the variance is explained. Positively associated with examination complexity are specialty practice, year of graduation, examination length, office equipment and examinations per week. Six of the eight professionalism measures relate to examination complexity in

Table 6.7 Regression analyses of examination length and examination complexity

	Examination Length		Examination Complexity	
	Unstandardized Regression Coefficient	*t* Statistic[a]	Unstandardized Regression Coefficient	*t* Statistic[a]
Control variables				
Patient income status	.489	1.037	.056	.798
Examination rooms	.252	1.212	−.040	−1.286
Overhead	.040	2.217	.000	.118
Examinations per week	−.173	−11.999	.004	1.703
Annual patient care hours	.001	1.264	−.000	−.812
Third party income	.015	.755	.005	1.633
Specialty practice	−.011	−.632	.008	3.480
Year of graduation	−.056	−2.533	.013	3.964
Office equipment	.448	1.980	.354	11.055
Examination length	. . .	. . .	.035	8.230
Examination complexity	1.579	8.286	. . .	. . .
Professionalism				
Legislated professionalism	.425	1.659	.037	.958
State AOA membership	.023	1.343	−.003	−1.066
Journals received	.167	.620	.101	2.534
Continuing education hours	.047	2.429	.010	3.498
AOA involvement	.228	1.939	.037	2.136
No advertising	1.252	1.342	−.152	−1.098
Separate service fee	.283	.550	.193	2.527
Anticommercialism score	.541	4.050	.034	1.722
Constant	16.493		−.084	

[a] t statistic of absolute value of 1.65 is significant at $P = 0.05$ in one-tailed test, 1.96 in two-tailed test. N = 1,193 and $\bar{R}^2 = 0.29$ for examination length; N = 1,194 and $\bar{R}^2 = 0.36$ for examination complexity. Means assigned to missing values of independent variables.

the anticipated positive direction, with five of the six statistically significant at the 0.05 level (the two negative coefficients are not statistically significant).

Interestingly, the indicators of state regulation and state AOA membership do not have strong effects on quality independent of the individual-level measures of professionalism, in contrast to the strong effect of both legislated professionalism and state AOA membership on price. Quality appears to vary more with individual characteristics, particularly continuing education and AOA involvement, while price seems to be relatively more of a product of market structure as measured by structural professionalism. This helps to explain why state average prices did not change substantially when adjusted for quality (and other factors) in tables 6.5 and 6.6.

Conclusions: Professionalism, Price, and Quality in Optometry

Several different methods of analysis have been employed to study the relationship between the price and quality of optometric services and professionalism. Consistently, the behavioral, attitudinal and structural measures of professionalism positively influence the price of optometric services, independent of their quality. State restrictions on optometric practice raise the price of services, and the requirement for continuing education is a particularly expensive one in terms of prices which optometrists charge.

At the same time, professionalism and the quality of services are positively related after controlling for the effect of several other variables on quality. This is particularly true for the individual-level measures of professionalism. Optometrists who behave and believe as "professionals" both charge higher prices and provide services which are longer and more technically complex. It is also reasonable to say in this case that the services are of higher quality. This is an important finding in light of the large number of studies showing that professionalism has negative consequences, because those studies rarely consider the consequences for the quality of services. At the very least the results indicate that failure to include measures of quality when attempting to explain price variations is a deficiency in past research, and the notion that increases in price reflect improved quality should not be dismissed.

The analyses conducted above do not definitively prove the existence of causal linkages between professionalism and price, professionalism and quality, and quality and price. However, it is fair to state that the evidence strongly suggests that professionalism raises prices, quality raises prices, and professionalism raises quality. The existence of an independent, positive direct effect of professionalism on price is of major importance, because it indicates the possibility that "self" rather than "public" interests are being served by professionalism.

Given the imperfect nature of the measures used here, no amount of analysis of the data can be fully conclusive. This analysis is limited by the use of indirect, self-reported quality measures. In addition, the chronological order of price and quality changes cannot be evaluated with the cross-sectional data used here. It is possible that quality (as measured here) may be raised only to justify higher prices, and the quality improvements are mere "window-dressing" with little relevance to the real needs of the consumer.

The analysis would prove more convincing if other measures of quality, such as patient outcomes, were available. The fact that there is some connection between quality as measured here and price should be encouraging to those who argue that more professional services are higher quality services, and the collection of other measures should be pursued. One such study of vision care services which uses different measures of quality is scheduled to be released by the FTC in 1980.

Similarly, it would be useful to have measures of prices which consumers pay for services, in addition to the prices which optometrists report that they charge.

Even with the limitations of the data collected here, it is possible to speculate on the size of price-quality trade-offs for optometric services. This can be done by interpreting the regression coefficients in table 6.4 as the expected change in examination price with a change of one unit in the quality variable, holding all other independent variables constant.[2] In table 6.4 the coefficients reveal a trade-off of $0.12 for an additional minute of examination length, $0.30 for an additional examination procedure and $0.54 for an additional item of equipment. An addition of, for example, ten minutes and one additional procedure to the average examination of an optometrist would result in approximately $2,500 per year more in income from examination prices (based on 1,645 examinations per year).

In addition to paying more for higher quality, consumers can expect to pay more for the services of a "professional"—an additional $0.40 for each unit of AOA involvement, for example, and $1.31 more for each unit of legislated professionalism in the state. As a result, average prices for an optometric examination can be expected to be about 25 percent higher in a state with all four items of legislated professionalism than a state with none of the items of legislated professionalism.

The continuing education requirement in states has a particularly large effect on price, with average prices $2.61 higher in states requiring continuing education. Based upon 16,000 optometrists in states which require continuing education, each providing 1,645 examinations yearly, the continuing education requirement may now be costing consumers almost $70 million yearly in higher examination prices only, independent of quality-induced price increases.[3] The total costs of the other state restrictions are smaller but are substantial and certainly worth further scrutiny as to their "public-interest" value.

Professionalism and the Public Interest

The belief that "optometry was created in the public interest," whether true or not, is shared deeply by virtually all members of the profession. This public-interest perspective is common to all of the professions, and it rests on the belief that professionalism has resulted in valuable gains in the quality of services performed by the occupation.

From another viewpoint, however, the professionalization of optometry and other occupations is characterized mainly by political battles to achieve an economic monopoly over a sector of the division of labor. The fifty-year struggle in optometry to eliminate the low-priced, high-volume producers labelled "commercialists" certainly lends itself to this interpretation. Such an interpretation of the process, however, is not sufficient evidence for labelling professionalization a "self-interest" activity. Optometrists would argue that they merely have been using all the legitimate tools of the political and economic systems to achieve the higher level of quality vision care they are seeking. In the end, an assessment of the public-interest value of the professions must rest on an evaluation of the consequences of professionalism, rather than its motivation.

The Effect of Professionalism on Price and Quality

Optometrists do seem to have some empirical support for the optimistic interpretation of their motives in professionalizing. The quality of vision services, at least as they define quality, does vary with the degree of professionalism of the practitioner. The evidence from this study suggests that professionalism in optometry has led to one probable public benefit—optometric services of greater complexity and length.

Quality, however, is but one aspect of the public interest in health and other professional services. Two other major elements of the public interest are the price and the accessibility of professional services. Based on the findings of this study, the professionalization efforts of optometrists have resulted in prices much higher than can be justified by higher quality levels. Quality-adjusted prices vary consistently and positively with levels of professionalism, implying either that professionalism allows the charging of a premium for services beyond their true market value, or that some unmeasured dimension of quality (which does not vary with the dimensions considered here) explains the price differentials. Professions will always advance the latter argument, but at a certain point consistently negative findings based on different measures of quality will make their claims unreasonable. This study joins the body of evidence implying that professions exploit their autonomous status by charging prices in excess of justified levels. This casts some doubt on the empirical reality of the "service orientation" attribute of professionals.

Higher prices in turn decrease the accessibility of services to consumers, since fewer services can be afforded. In the provision of optometric services, higher prices probably decrease demand to a greater degree than for many other medical services, because there are substitutes for optometrists (ophthalmologists and opticians) and because vision examinations are a "luxury" item for low income consumers, as are extra eyeglasses, tinted lenses, stylish frames, etc., for most consumers. Although his results are ambiguous, Coate's (1974) analysis suggests that price elasticities of demand for optometric services are negative and are higher than those estimated for physician services. Benham and Benham (1975) discover large negative price elasticities in their eyeglass study, with a 30 percent increase in price implying about a 30 percent decrease in the proportion of people obtaining eyeglasses. Due to the positive influence of quality on price, higher quality levels also will contribute to lower accessibility. In addition, to the extent that producing additional quality takes more time, producers will offer fewer services per capita. In general, increases in the quality of services are likely to raise absolute prices and decrease accessibility.

The price-quality-accessibility trade-offs made in the process of professionalization are illustrated clearly in the case of the decision made by optometry to eliminate higher volume, lower price "commercial" services. As defined by "employment in a profit-making form," there are very few commercialists in optometry today. Only 30 optometrists (2.5 percent of survey respondents) were so employed. These 30 commercialists charge an average examination price of $18.02, compared to $24.53 for the remainder of the respondents. They average 47.67 examinations per week, compared to 33.54 (differences significant at $P < 0.001$). The commercialists indeed do produce lower price, higher volume service. The quality of their services, however is lower when defined by examination length (24.17 minutes compared to 33.58 minutes), office equipment (2.83 compared to 4.09), and examination complexity (3.23 compared to 4.36)—all differences significant at $P < 0.001$.

But has the public interest really been served by the decision to eliminate commercialism in optometry? Probably not, although the answer requires further information on what minimum quality level consumers will accept. In the past, decisions about minimum quality levels have been made internally within occupations, and political resources of competing intra-occupational segments have determined the outcomes (e.g., the Flexner Report reforms in medicine). In optometry, commercial optometrists in most states have been unable to match the political strength of the professional segment of the occupation. Because of the particular ethic that is the basis of professionalism, regulatory decisions by professional segments of occupations will be biased in the direction of too-high quality levels.

The Quality-at-any-Cost Ethic of the Professions

For several reasons, professionals left to themselves will be likely to make decisions in favor of higher quality without seriously considering the impact on price or accessibility. No doubt most professionals will argue that it is their mandate to provide the highest quality service possible, irrespective of price, for quality improvement is the basic rationale for professionalization. This position was illustrated earlier in a selection from an introductory textbook for optometry students (Hirsch and Wick, 1968:202), and the quality service ethic is a major product of the professional socialization process. Health professionals deal with patients on an individual basis, and their ethical commitment is to treat the individual patient with the highest quality service available, regardless of price. Referring to physicians, Havighurst (1977b:38) observes that "In general, the prevailing professional view, maintained in large part as a matter of ethics, is that quality of care is the profession's business alone, that there is only one acceptable standard, and that cost has nothing to do with it." For professionals, price is not explicitly included in their notion of the "public interest." A typical statement which exemplifies this ethic in operation in optometry is as follows: "Consumerism cannot mean price above all but value received for value offered. If price is to be paramount, let the buyer beware . . . for a few dollars saved at the cost of less than the best in quality eye care is usually more expensive in the long run. Human vision is much too precious to put on the market place. There are no bargains in quality care" (Eger, 1975:581).

When faced with a decision involving the quality of services, professionals are in a no-lose situation: to be true to their ethical standards they must increase quality, and because of the structural position of the professions, this quality increase in turn augments their self-interest. A result of this process of justification is higher prices for the consumer and increased income or a lower quantity output of services for the practitioner.

Professions can and often do have idealistic motivations for making decisions in favor of professional restrictiveness, which explains their almost rabid defense of their past activities. Yet their decisions often fail to serve the public interest because they ignore the issues of price and accessibility of services. The public interest demands that decisions be made on the basis of the price-quality-accessibility trade-offs; the professions demand that they be made solely on the basis of quality. Yet this is only one important feature of the current system. Not only are professional regulatory decisions made primarily on the basis of their effect on quality, but quality is defined in particular ways which favor the continuation of professionalism.

Who Defines Quality?

The question of "Who defines quality?" was not even asked until recent challenges to professionalism developed; previously it was assumed that only the involved profession could make judgments about what levels of quality should be allowed. The problem with this assumption is that professions will tend to define quality in particular ways—ways that they can control. Thus professions define quality in terms of educational level, test performance, attendance at continuing education, and technical sophistication of treatment procedures. Newer equipment by definition is of higher quality than older equipment; more complicated procedures are of higher quality than simpler ones; longer educational training is superior to shorter training, etc. If quality were determined by outcomes, professions would lose some control over their destiny.

Physicians find it easier to argue their superiority over family nurse practitioners, for example, on the basis of educational level rather than relative outcomes of their services.

In a perceptive discussion of innovation in health care, Benham (1978) contends that health professions will act to stifle innovations that threaten their monopoly positions, while encouraging those that improve the "quality" of services. Innovative health care delivery is discouraged by regulations against advertising, corporate employment, mercantile location, etc., because those forms of delivery necessarily lead to violation of professionally defined quality standards. At the extreme, this process leads to an identity of professionalism and quality; by definition, if one is not a professional, one provides low quality care. Such a process clearly is at work in optometry; note the following quotation from a 1953 speech by the president of the American Optometric Association (JFOA, 1954:3): "We must direct attention to the professional method which has proved to be the only effective method of providing adequate vision care. . . . Give the patient the thorough examination, the professional attention, the unquestionable materials that distinguish the highest type of professional optometry."

As definers of quality, professions will neglect the fact that the worst level of quality service for consumers is no service at all. Restrictions on entry, mobility, and types of practice, and a miscellany of other prohibitions, may be administered by most professions with the sincere and idealistic goal of increasing quality. But the restrictions also reduce the supply of providers and raise prices. Nevertheless, it is very unlikely that the profession would agree that more practitioners, more conveniently located (e.g., in shopping centers), might be worth the sacrifice of "x" units of a mean quality measure for practitioners in the occupation. The power of the professions to define quality contributes to what is known as the Cadillac effect—limited, high quality services available only to high income consumers.

Finally, the question "Who defines quality?" is of significance because definitions of quality can become the lever with which professions manipulate the supply of competitors. Ophthalmologists do not mobilize against attempts by optometrists to gain the legal right to prescribe drugs until they feel economically threatened by competition (Begun and Lippincott, 1980). Similarly, we may expect dentists' opposition to denturists, physicians' opposition to nurse practitioners, psychiatrists' opposition to psychologists, etc., to grow in proportion to the economic threat which the upcoming group presents. The surface argument of all the higher status participants in these conflicts is that "my quality is higher than yours, and consumers will be endangered if you are allowed to supply my services." At the least, we can never take those statements at face value, and research on the quality-of-care should be a major agendum in the public challenge to professionalism. In the next section, such research is described in more detail, and other suggestions for future research are given.

Future Research

There is an obvious need for occupation-specific research on the minimum level of service quality that is acceptable to consumers. For example, if vision examinations averaging fifteen minutes instead of thirty, including three procedures instead of four, are not dangerous to the consumer, those vision examinations should be in the marketplace competing, at a lower price, with the longer and more complex examinations. Obviously, one cannot ask only the most professional members of an occupation to make these judgments; that is what is wrong with the current system. In the well-established, relatively homogeneous professions, efforts would need to be expended to solicit quality judgments of less traditional practitioners.

Much research, particularly by economists on the subject of regulation, is based on either a self-interest (capture) theory or public-interest theory of regulation. In reality, regulation serves multiple interests, and the task of theory should be to predict what the particular configuration of interests served will be, and under what conditions. Leffler (1978) reaches this conclusion in his analysis of some of the consequences of regulation of the supply of physicians; he finds consequences beneficial to both physicians and consumers.

Similar implications for sociological theory can be drawn. In chapter 2 the functionalist and power approaches to the study of professionalism were reviewed. Neither approach is comprehensive. The functionalist assumption that professionals are characterized by a service orientation is challenged by the evidence from this and other studies, although under certain conditions such an orientation may be present. The power theory, which centers on the achievement of professionalism by political domination, should be extended to predict the consequences of such political success for consumers. In certain situations, for example, when the professionalization movement is guided by lay policy-makers rather than the affected occupation (White, 1979), it may be more beneficial to consumers.

Asserting the Public Interest Through Public Policy

The analysis of professionalism, price, and quality in optometry reveals two basic public policy problems that should be confronted:

Professionals left to themselves will not give serious consideration to price and access issues when faced with decisions that will affect the quality of services.

Professionalism leads to higher prices, independent of quality.

An obvious strategy for addressing the first problem is to involve nonprofessionals in the decisions that affect the price, quality, and accessibility of professional services. The "quality-at-any-cost" position asserted by professionals is too narrow to include all components of the public interest. This is not unusual or unexpected; MacRae (1976:28;1977), for example, has observed that "The ethical standards and alternatives with which members of a profession face questions of public policy are . . . unavoidably narrow" and a general ethical perspective is hardly to be expected from a profession. More attention to ethical issues in the professional socialization process would be helpful, but it would be difficult and perhaps unwise to widen the ethical perspective of health professionals. The disadvantages of destroying the quality ethic are substantial; it would be preferable for health professionals to continue to exercise the ethic but within constraints set by society and its more comprehensive view of the public interest.

Although directly affected by the price, quality, and accessibility of health services, consumers typically have not been involved in political decisions over professional regulatory issues. The reason can be found in the depth of the consumer's interest in each separate professional regulation issue, relative to the interest of the profession involved. Olson (1965) and Stigler (1971) discuss this fact in more theoretical terms. Additionally, political scientists point out that groups seeking governmental largesse in the self-regulatory arena "will strive to keep these conflicts privatized, often succeeding in keeping the 'audience' unaware that a conflict even exists" (Hayes, 1978:156).

Structural changes, some already in progress, can widen the opportunity for consumer interests to be expressed more effectively. The major tool of the quality control process is the state licensing board, commonly composed of members of the regulated occupation who are selected by the state professional association. Movements are underway to place consumers on these boards; in optometry, thirteen states have lay members on their optometric licensing board (AOA, 1978). More meaningful would be total control of the board by consumers or bureaucrats, with consultation available from an advisory panel of practitioners who are randomly selected or assigned by quota to ensure representation of "less professional" elements. The argument that nonprofessionals cannot judge the quality of services is valid to some extent, but professionals must learn to function as consultants who provide information to decision-makers who have a more general ethical perspective.

Public control of licensing boards would not only broaden their ethical perspective; in addition, public control would decrease the apparent ease with which professions can reap monopoly profits through anticompetitive regulations and thus would address the second policy problem mentioned above. Realistically, of course, the long-term experience of "independent" regulatory units suggests the likelihood of co-optation by the regulated group (Pfeffer, 1974a), so the impact of such a policy change would probably be small.

Because it will be difficult to conduct required quality-of-care studies of professions without the cooperation of the relevant profession, it may be desirable to statutorily encourage such studies by requiring "price-quality-accessibility" impact statements by professional regulatory boards on proposed (and current) regulations. This at least would have the effect of forcing the professions to publicly debate and justify their positions. To a degree, this is already occurring in health systems agencies, which must approve large capital expansions of hospital facilities, and in sunset commission hearings, which often debate the public-interest value of various professional regulations. The sunset laws passed in several states are a healthy trend because they place the burden of proof on the profession itself to justify its restrictive rules, thus encouraging quality-of-care studies. However, sunset commissions are likely to have little success in altering licensing laws of the major health professions because of the political power of the professions, especially at the state and local levels (Rubin, 1980).

The independent effect of professionalism on price can be considered a monopoly benefit, so that stimulation of competition among and within health professions is another appropriate public policy response to that problem. Consumers must be given the information and ability to purchase lower priced and lower quality care if they so desire. This alternative is exemplified by the FTC and Department of Justice initiatives reviewed in chapter 1 to open the professional market to greater competition by eliminating several restrictions on entry and types of practice in the professions. The agencies have acted to legalize price advertising by professionals, for example, decreasing consumer ignorance in the market for professional services. As Beales (1980) observes, however, removal of advertising restrictions may not stimulate advertising due to peer group pressures, and it will also be necessary to legalize employment of professionals by nonprofessional corporations and/or nonprofessional ownership of professional firms. As a further pro-competition policy, Havighurst (1977b:38) would increase consumer choices for alternative sources of health care services, such as health maintenance organizations. More vigorous enforcement of antitrust laws against the professions also would be part of a pro-competition strategy. For example, a strong case can be made that relative value scales of medical services, which can be used to fix prices, inhibit competition among private third-party payers in the development of cost-containment strategies and among physicians in the setting of fees (Havighurst and Kissam, 1979).

Greater competition can be achieved without removing all minimum standards for health care practitioners. A reasonable first step would be greater reliance on certification mechanisms short of licensure, such as registration or voluntary certification. If research determines that licensure is justified, minimum quality standards based on processes (e.g., record-keeping requirements, minimum examination requirements) or on outcomes (e.g., patient complaints, treatment successes) would be preferable to the overkill in the current system which raises entry standards to extreme levels. Hershey (1976) has proposed a system of institutional licensure, which would terminate individual occupational licensing boards and assign institutions the responsibility for determining qualifications and maintaining the competence of their personnel. While mini-hierarchies in institutions would likely mirror the current macro-hierarchy of control within and among professions, the chances for innovative change would multiply greatly.

Public policy-makers may be unable to resist the political pressures of the professions' quality-at-any-cost ethic. Havighurst (1977a) makes the point that private organizations such as insurance companies are not as susceptible to political pressure as public agencies and thus will have more "rational" views of price-quality-accessibility trade-offs: "Private decision-makers with an immediate interest in control are less apt to collapse in the face of an unsubstantiated quality-of-care claim than is a public decision-maker, who is usually in a position to commit the public's money to keep his conscience clear and protect his political image by resolving all plausible doubts in favor of more and better health services. . . . Private-sector initiatives . . . are more likely to address the many trade-offs on their merits . . ." (Havighurst, 1977a:481). The realities of legislative decision-making in the states, where most professional regulatory policies are set, illustrate Havighurst's concerns. Begun and Feldman (1979) find that state political systems with low interparty competition, low state policy innovativeness, and high turnover among legislators are more likely to grant the restrictive laws requested by professional optometry. Just as some private-sector groups should be more likely to assess regulatory issues on their merits, so also should federal agencies like the FTC and Department of Justice, who are slightly more isolated from political pressures than are state legislators. Their investigations should receive full support, and similar actions by other federal agencies, especially those with research resources, should be stimulated.

Most of the strategies mentioned above would help to fragment the demand pattern for regulatory policy and would contribute to a system of countervailing powers acting in the political environment. Some fragmentation of interests should be achieved naturally as the complexity of the structure of health care delivery grows and health occupations multiply in number, making it increasingly likely that newly professionalizing health occupations will encounter opposition regarding the boundaries of their work domain (e.g., family nurse practitioners versus physicians). Fragmentation in the political environment will mean that state legislators can no longer safely just ratify the unchallenged positions of professional group members.

It is not necessary to fault the professions for the dilemma faced by contemporary public policy. In fact, society has neglected its role in enforcing the public interest—professionals have behaved as we should have expected them to behave. They have acted to raise the quality of their services by making decisions which in turn raise prices and decrease access to services. The decisions are not made solely on the basis of the profit motive or the self-interest of the professional. They are based instead on the particular view of the public interest which professionals espouse; that view is focused on the individual client and his/her need for the highest quality service. Society must reassert its broader, collective view of the public interest by placing external constraints on the ability of professions to increase quality and to reap monopolistic returns. As stated by Tuohy (1976:679-80), "Governments cannot continue to expect that coherent public policy can be achieved by dealing with professional groups as if they were the 'owners' of their respective technologies . . . Governments must come to treat professional technologies as *public* property and must assume authority over the management of that property." The quality of professional services is public property because it is developed under an exchange agreement with government. Government simply has neglected to enforce the agreement to date. The alternative to challenging professionalism in the technologically advancing field of health services is a society in which only wealthy consumers can afford high quality health care, or in which societal resources are drained by the health services sector.

Appendix A
Comparison of Characteristics of Respondents to 1976 National Survey of the Optometric Profession with Total Active Optometrists in 1973

Table A1 Percent distribution of 1976 survey respondents and 1973 total active optometrists by sex, age, and race

	1973 Total Active Optometrists (N = 19,265)	1976 Survey Respondents (N = 1,195)
Age		
<30 years	8.8	7.5
30–39 years	16.0	22.8
40–49 years	27.4	20.1
50–59 years	32.4	34.0
60–69 years	11.3	11.9
70+ years	4.1	2.3
Not reported	0.0	1.4
Total	100.0	100.0

Note: $\chi^2 = 68.22$, d.f. = 5, $P<0.01$. χ^2 computed on frequencies, excluding "not reported."

Sex		
Male	97.9	98.7
Female	2.1	1.3
Total	100.0	100.0

Note: $\chi^2 = 3.51$, d.f. = 1, $P<0.10$. χ^2 computed on frequencies.

Race		
White	96.8	97.1
Black	0.5	0.4
Asian/Oriental	1.5	1.7
Other	0.4	0.6
Not reported	0.7	0.3
Total	99.9	100.0

Note: $\chi^2 = 1.08$, d.f. = 3, $P<0.80$. χ^2 computed on frequencies, excluding "not reported."

Source: OMRP, 1976: Tables 13, 16b, 23.

Table A2 Percent distribution of 1976 survey respondents and 1973 total active optometrists by optometry school

Optometry School	1973 Total Active Optometrists (N = 19,265)	1976 Survey Respondents (N = 1,195)
Northern Illinois	21.2	14.6
Southern (Memphis)	13.9	17.0
Pennsylvania	12.9	13.1
Southern California (Los Angeles)	7.9	7.7
New England (Massachusetts)	6.3	6.2
Illinois	6.2	9.2
Ohio State University	5.3	6.8
Pacific University	5.2	6.9
Chicago (Monroe)	4.7	3.4
University of California (Berkeley)	4.5	5.0
Columbia	4.2	2.6
University of Houston	2.2	3.7
Indiana University	2.0	2.8
Other	2.6	0.9
Not reported	0.8	0.2
Total	99.9	100.1

Source: OMRP, 1976: Table 30.
Note: $\chi^2 = 97.14$, d.f. = 13, $P<0.01$. χ^2 computed on frequencies, excluding "not reported."

Table A3 Percent distribution of 1976 survey respondents and 1973 total active optometrists by principal form of employment

Principal Form of Employment	1973 Total Active Optometrists (N = 19,265)	1976 Survey Respondents (N = 1,195)
Self-employed in solo practice	61.7	64.5
Self-employed in partnership or group, or partner in professional corporation	19.7	28.0
Employed by profit-making firm	2.2	2.5
Employed by federal government	2.3	0.3
Other	9.9	4.4
Not reported	4.2	0.3
Total	100.0	100.0

Source: OMRP, 1976: Table 38.
Note: χ^2 = 90.92, d.f. = 4, $P<0.01$. χ^2 computed on frequencies, excluding "not reported."

Table A4 Percent distribution of 1976 survey respondents and 1973 total active optometrists by geographic division

Geographic Division	Total Active Optometrists, 1973 (N = 19,265)	1976 Survey Respondents (N = 1,195)
New England	7.2	6.9
Middle Atlantic	17.6	15.2
East North Central	22.1	20.3
West North Central	8.6	9.7
South Atlantic	11.4	12.6
East South Central	4.6	4.4
West South Central	7.7	9.0
Mountain	4.1	5.0
Pacific	16.6	16.7
Total	99.9	99.8

Source: OMRP, 1976: Table 6.
Note: χ^2 = 13.91, d.f. = 8, $P<0.10$. χ^2 computed on frequencies.

Appendix B

NATIONAL SURVEY OF THE
OPTOMETRIC PROFESSION

This questionnaire is designed to help study the extent of professional development in optometry and the factors responsible for that development. The study is being conducted by staff from the Health Services Research Center of the University of North Carolina from July 1976 to July 1977.

The questionnaire will take about fifteen minutes to complete. It includes a minimum of questions pertinent to your background, attitudes, and practice. Response categories have been provided for your convenience and in order to maximize anonymity. You may find that a question or the response categories do not fit your own particular situation as accurately as you could describe it. If so, you are encouraged to use the margin for additional comments or explanation.

You have been selected at random as a representative of other optometrists, and it is important that we receive completed questionnaires from all of those in the sample. Please return your completed questionnaire in the enclosed stamped envelope within *two weeks* after you have received the questionnaire.

We invite your response with the assurance that it will be completely *CONFIDENTIAL*, as we realize the sensitivity of some of the questions. Except for the identification number to enable us to keep track of questionnaires as they are returned, your identity will not be known to the researchers. Your name and address will be destroyed when a complete questionnaire is returned, and therefore your response will be anonymous.

If we can answer questions or be of assistance, please contact the director of the study:

James W. Begun, M.A.
Health Services Research Center
The University of North Carolina at Chapel Hill
Division of Health Affairs, Building 207 H
Chapel Hill, NC 27514
Telephone (919) 966-1388

ATTITUDES

We are interested in your opinion about several current issues in the professional development of optometry. Please record your opinion on the following statements by *checking one space* for each statement.

	Strongly Agree	Agree	Neutral	Disagree	Strongly Disagree
1. I have satisfactory working relationships with opticians in my area. (Check here if *no* opticians in area _____ .)					
2. I have satisfactory working relationships with ophthalmologists.					
3. Persons in the profession of optometry maintain a high degree of idealism.					
4. The scope of optometry should be expanded to include the use of *therapeutic* pharmaceutical agents.					
5. Employment of optometrists in commercial establishments should be permitted.					
6. In general, the practice of non-dispensing optometry should be encouraged by the profession.					
The profession should require continued education of optometrists.					
8. Any weakening of this profession would be harmful to the public.					
9. The public would benefit by the price advertising of *ophthalmic materials* by optometrists.					
10. The public would benefit by the price advertising of *professional services* by optometrists.					
11. I would leave my profession if my net income were reduced by twenty-five percent.					
12. The American Optometric Association represents my opinions on most issues related to optometry.					
13. The benefits that society receives from optometry are under-estimated by most members of the public.					

14. If price advertising of ophthalmic materials by optometrists were common, would you advertise?

1 _____ Yes

2 _____ Possibly

3 _____ No _____▶ If no, why not? _____

_____

_____

15. Do you consider yourself conservative, moderate, or liberal in your political thinking?

1 _____ conservative

2 _____ moderate

3 _____ liberal

16. Of the following three possible reasons for practicing optometry, which do you feel is most important to you? least important?

a. *MOST IMPORTANT* (check one)   b. *LEAST IMPORTANT* (check one)

1 _____ chance to help people   1 _____ chance to help people

2 _____ economic opportunity   2 _____ economic opportunity

3 _____ technical content of work   3 _____ technical content of work

CURRENT PROFESSIONAL ACTIVITIES

These questions relate to your involvement in several professional activities.

17. How many approved hours of continuing education credit do you expect to complete during 1976?

_____ hours

18. Do you receive any of the following journals? (check all that apply)

a. _____ Journal of the American Optometric Association

b. _____ American Journal of Optometry and Physiological Optics

c. _____ The Optical Journal and Review of Optometry

d. _____ Optometric Management

e. _____ Optometric Weekly

f. _____ American Journal of Public Health

19. Have you enrolled in a transcript quality course in pharmacology since your graduation from optometry school?

    1 _____ Yes

    2 _____ No

20. Have you had a satisfactory relationship with your state board of optometric examiners?

    1 _____ Yes

    2 _____ No _____➤ If no, what problems have occurred, and when?

    _____

    _____

    _____

21. Have you had a satisfactory relationship with your AOA-affiliated state optometric association?

    1 _____ Yes

    2 _____ No _____➤ If no, what problems have occurred, and when?

    _____

    _____

    _____

22. Are you a member of any of the following groups? (check all that apply)

    a. _____ American Optometric Association (AOA)

    b. _____ state optometric association affiliated with AOA

    c. _____ local or district optometric association affiliated with AOA

    d. _____ state optometric association *not* affiliated with AOA

       (please record name of association here _____)

    e. _____ National Optometric Association

    f. _____ American Academy of Optometry

    g. _____ Optometric Extension Program Foundation, Inc.

23. Do you regularly attend meetings of any of the following groups? (check all that apply)

   a. _____ American Optometric Association (AOA)

   b. _____ state optometric association affiliated with AOA

   c. _____ local or district optometric association affiliated with AOA

   d. _____ state optometric association *not* affiliated with AOA

       (please record name of association here _____)

   e. _____ National Optometric Association

   f. _____ American Academy of Optometry

   g. _____ Optometric Extension Program Foundation, Inc.

24. Do you hold or have you held offices or committee positions in any of the following groups? (check all that apply)

   a. _____ state board of optometric examiners

   b. _____ American Optometric Association (AOA)

   c. _____ state optometric association affiliated with AOA

   d. _____ local or district optometric association affiliated with AOA

   e. _____ state optometric association *not* affiliated with AOA

       (please record name of association here _____)

   f. _____ National Optometric Association

   g. _____ American Academy of Optometry

   h. _____ Optometric Extension Program Foundation, Inc.

BACKGROUND

Next are some questions about personal characteristics, your educational background, and your optometric practice.

25. Your sex

   1 _____ Male

   2 _____ Female

26. Your race/ethnicity

    1 _____ White

    2 _____ Black

    3 _____ Asian/Oriental

    4 _____ Other

27. In what year were you born? _____
    (Year)

28. What is the exact name of the optometry school or other institution at which you received your optometric education?

    _____   _____
    (Name of School)   (State)

29. In what year did you graduate from the above school?   19 ____

30. How many years of *college* or *university* education have you had *in addition to* optometry school? (check one)

    _____ 0 years   _____ 5 years

    _____ 1 year   _____ 6 years

    _____ 2 years   _____ 7 years

    _____ 3 years   _____ 8 or more years

    _____ 4 years

31. How many hours do you spend in the following optometric activities in a typical workweek?

    a. _____ hours optometric patient care ——————▶ | If 0 hours in optometric patient care, STOP! Rest of questionnaire does not apply. Please *return* questionnaire in enclosed stamped envelope. Thank you.

    b. _____ hours optometric teaching

    c. _____ hours optometric research

    d. _____ hours other optometric activity (school administration, work for associations, etc.)

32. How many weeks do you expect to work in the above activities in 1976 (excluding vacation)?

    _____ weeks

33. What is your principal form of employment? (check one)

1 _____ Self-employed in solo practice

2 _____ Self-employed in partnership or group practice,
or partner in a professional corporation_____ ➤ | How many other optometrists are in the practice? _____ |

3 _____ Employed by profit-making firm

4 _____ Employed by Federal Government

5 _____ Other (please specify _____)

34. Approximately what percentage of your optometric patient care activity is spent in the following types of care?

a. _____ % General practice

b. _____ % Contact lenses

c. _____ % Visual training/orthoptics

d. _____ % Other specialty
100% Total optometric patient care activity

35. In what state(s) do you hold an active license?

_____
Name of state(s)

36. In what state is your primary practice located?

_____
Name of state

37. What is the population of the community in which your primary practice is located?

1 _____ 500,000 or more

2 _____ 100,000 - 499,999

3 _____ 25,000 - 99,999

4 _____ 10,000 - 24,999

5 _____ under 10,000

38. Do you (or your group) practice in more than one location (in one or more branch offices)?

1 _____ Yes_____ ➤ If yes, in how many total locations? _____

2 _____ No

PATIENT SERVICE AREA CHARACTERISTICS

This section asks for information about the type of patients you serve.

"PATIENT SERVICE AREA" refers to the region for which you *routinely* provide services.

39. Approximately how many ophthalmologists are in your "patient service area"?

    _____ Ophthalmologists

40. Approximately how many dispensing opticians are in your "patient service area"?

    _____ Dispensing opticians

41. Approximately how many other optometrists are in your "patient service area"?

    _____ Optometrists

42. How would you describe the economic status of the *majority* of your patients? (check one)

    1 _____ High income (over $15,000)

    2 _____ Moderate income ($10,000 - $15,000)

    3 _____ Low income (under $10,000)

43. Approximately what are the racial/ethnic characteristics of the patients you treat?

    a. _____ % White

    b. _____ % Black

    c. _____ % Asian/Oriental

    d. _____ % Other
       100% Total

44. What is the approximate percentage of your practice income resulting from Medicaid (Title XIX)?

    _____ % Medicaid

45. What is the approximate percentage of your practice income resulting from other third party payment, such as vision service group, insurance, or government programs other than Medicaid?

    _____ % Other third party

PRACTICE CHARACTERISTICS

The remainder of the questionnaire asks about several characteristics of your patient care practice.

46. Do you disclose prices for frames over the telephone?

 1 _____ Yes, always

 2 _____ Yes, sometimes

 3 _____ No

47. Do you separate charges for materials from professional fees?

 1 _____ Yes, always

 2 _____ Yes, but only on request

 3 _____ No

48. Do you provide patients with copies of spectacle lens prescriptions?

 1 _____ Yes, always

 2 _____ Yes, but only on request

 3 _____ No

49. Do you use the following *diagnostic* pharmaceutical agents in your practice when appropriate?

 a. *Fluorescein*   1 _____ Yes

         2 _____ No

 c. *Mydriatics, miotics, or cycloplegics*   1 _____ Yes

 b. *Topical anesthetics*   1 _____ Yes   2 _____ No

         2 _____ No

50. Do you use *therapeutic* pharmaceutical agents in your practice?

 1 _____ Yes

 2 _____ No

51. In 1976, has the availability of your services been advertised in the media (excluding announcement of new office openings, and Yellow Pages)?

 1 _____ Yes ⮕ If yes, number of advertisements _____

 2 _____ No

52. In 1976, has the *price* of your materials or services been advertised in the media?

 1 _____ Yes ⮕ If yes, number of advertisements _____

 2 _____ No

53. In 1976, has any other facet of your optometric practice been advertised in the media?

 1 _____ Yes _____ If yes, please specify subject of advertisement _____

 2 _____ No

54. In your optometric practice, how many non-optometrists (including secretaries, opticians, paraoptometric personnel, etc.) are employed to assist you?

 a. _____ Full-time (35 hours or more per week) non-optometrists

 b. _____ Part-time (less than 35 hours per week) non-optometrists

55. Do you share these personnel with associates?

 1 _____ Yes _____ If yes, with how many associates do you share
                      these personnel? _____ associates
 2 _____ No

56. Estimate how many patients you provide care for in a typical full workweek.

 _____ patients per week

57. Approximately what percentage of these patients are presbyopic?

 _____ % presbyopic

58. Estimate how many complete examinations/vision analyses you perform in a typical full workweek.

 _____ examinations/vision analyses per week

59. Approximately what percentage of your complete examinations/visual analyses result in new prescriptions?

 _____ %

60. In a typical full workweek, how many patients do you refer to physicians?

 _____ referrals

61. How many examining rooms are in your primary practice office? (Include contact lens and visual training rooms.)

 _____ examining rooms

62. Which of the following equipment is available for use in your primary practice office? (check all that apply)

 a. _____ retinoscope   g. _____ ophthalmoscope

 b. _____ instrument for visual fields   h. _____ vision skills tester

 c. _____ phoropter   i. _____ intraocular pressure
                                                       instrument
 d. _____ ophthalmometer/keratometer
                                                  j. _____ sub-normal vision
 e. _____ sphygmomanometer   lenses

 f. _____ slit lamp

63. Which of the following procedures are routinely performed in a complete examination/visual analysis for a *presbyope* in your practice? (check all that apply)

a. _____ Complete case history

b. _____ Direct ophthalmoscopy

c. _____ Indirect ophthalmoscopy

d. _____ Evaluation of accommodation

e. _____ Phorias

f. _____ Ductions

g. _____ Blood pressure

h. _____ Examination of ocular media

i. _____ Recording cup/disc ratio

j. _____ Intraocular pressure

k. _____ Visual fields screening

l. _____ Biomicroscopy

m. _____ Refraction

n. _____ Visual acuity with *and* without correction

64. What is the approximate length of a complete examination/visual analysis for a *presbyope* in your practice? (check one)

01 _____ 1-10 minutes

02 _____ 11-15 minutes

03 _____ 16-20 minutes

04 _____ 21-25 minutes

05 _____ 26-30 minutes

06 _____ 31-35 minutes

07 _____ 36-40 minutes

08 _____ 41-45 minutes

09 _____ 46-50 minutes

10 _____ 51-55 minutes

11 _____ 56-60 minutes

12 _____ more than 60 minutes

65. What is your approximate charge for a complete examination/visual analysis for a presbyope? (Exclude material and material services.)

01 _____ $5.00-9.99

02 _____ $10.00-14.99

03 _____ $15.00-19.99

04 _____ $20.00-24.99

05 _____ $25.00-29.99

06 _____ $30.00-34.99

07 _____ $35.00-39.99

08 _____ $40.00-49.99

09 _____ $50.00 or more

10 _____ no charge (e.g., military, pre-paid practice)

66. What is your approximate charge for one pair of bifocal lenses? (Assume standard size, first division, corrected curve, untinted glass. Exclude material services.)

01 _____ $5.00-14.99

02 _____ $15.00-19.99

03 _____ $20.00-24.99

04 _____ $25.00-29.99

05 _____ $30.00-34.99

06 _____ $35.00-39.99

07 _____ $40.00-44.99

08 _____ $45.00-49.99

09 _____ $50.00-59.99

10 _____ $60.00-69.99

11 _____ $70.00 or more

12 _____ no charge (e.g., military)

13 _____ do not dispense

67. What is your approximate charge for a man's traditional plastic frame, such as the Stadium by American Optical or the Burbank by Bausch and Lomb?

01 _____ $5.00-9.99   07 _____ $35.00-39.99

02 _____ $10.00-14.99   08 _____ $40.00-49.99

03 _____ $15.00-19.99   09 _____ $50.00 or more

04 _____ $20.00-24.99   10 _____ no charge (e.g., military)

05 _____ $25.00-29.99   11 _____ do not dispense

06 _____ $30.00-34.99

68. What is the approximate *gross* income before taxes you expect to receive from *optometric practice* only during 1976? (If partner, use prorated portion of total practice. If employee, check here _____ .)

01 _____ $0-9,999   11 _____ $100,000-109,999

02 _____ $10,000-19,999   12 _____ $110,000-119,999

03 _____ $20,000-29,999   13 _____ $120,000-129,999

04 _____ $30,000-39,999   14 _____ $130,000-139,999

05 _____ $40,000-49,999   15 _____ $140,000-149,999

06 _____ $50,000-59,999   16 _____ $150,000-174,999

07 _____ $60,000-69,999   17 _____ $175,000-199,999

08 _____ $70,000-79,999   18 _____ $200,000-249,999

09 _____ $80,000-89,999   19 _____ $250,000-299,999

10 _____ $90,000-99,999   20 _____ $300,000 or more

69. Approximately what percentage of your expected 1976 *gross* income from optometric practice will be spent on overhead (wages, rent, lab, etc.)? (If employee, skip this question.)

_____ %

Please relate any comments or concerns raised by particular questions or the study as a whole.

_____

_____

_____

_____

_____

THANK YOU VERY MUCH

PLEASE MAIL THE QUESTIONNAIRE IN THE ENCLOSED STAMPED ENVELOPE

Appendix C

Table C1 Table of means and standard deviations (N = 1,195)

Variable	Mean	S.D.	Missing Cases
Examination price	24.353	7.200	13
Patient income status	1.958	.545	15
Urbanization	73.677	25.190	50
Frame price	17.257	4.748	76
Lens price	35.888	10.750	89
Examination rooms	2.189	1.327	7
Overhead	53.901	15.059	182
Examinations per week	33.944	18.958	45
Annual patient care hours	1856.391	401.518	35
Third party income	9.499	12.984	34
Specialty practice	19.938	17.038	1
Year of graduation	55.850	12.123	20
Examination length	33.335	9.947	2
Examination complexity	4.328	1.558	1
Office equipment	4.057	1.435	0
Legislated professionalism	2.866	.963	0
State AOA membership	71.323	15.190	0
Journals received	2.606	.986	6
Continuing education hours	21.508	14.110	32
AOA involvement	4.622	2.577	0
No advertising	.918	.275	5
Separate service fee	.566	.496	28
Anticommercialism score	9.947	2.022	28
Legislated professionalism components			
Continuing education required	.859	.348	0
O.D. advertising prohibited	.807	.395	0
Optician advertising prohibited	.562	.496	0
Mercantile location restricted	.638	.481	0

Notes

Chapter 1

1. For example, *Eckerd Optical Centers, Inc. v. Florida State Board of Dispensing Opticians*, 2nd Circuit Court, Florida (January 12, 1976); *Wall and Ochs v. State Board of Opticians*, Eastern District Court, North Carolina (April 5, 1979).

Chapter 4

1. Optometrists listed in *The Blue Book of Optometrists* (Professional Press, 1976) were hand counted in order to eliminate "retired" and multiply listed optometrists. *The Blue Book* listing was compiled prior to 1976, while AOA membership counts are for July, 1976. As a result, membership percentages are slightly overestimated.

2. The reliability coefficient for this score is of "modest" size. Nunnally (1967:226) points out that "In the early stages of research . . . reliabilities of .60 or .50 will suffice."

Chapter 5

1. This approach is consistent, although at a fairly primitive level methodologically, with Hall's (1979) discussion of the "social construction of the professions" and the significant role of aspiring occupations in defining what is considered "professional."

2. The variable "hours of continuing education credit received in 1976" has measurement error because some optometrists included large numbers of credit hours received for pharmacology courses that generally are taken once by practitioners who wish to use pharmaceutical agents in their practice and who are not recent optometry school graduates. Because the pharmacology courses were offered in only a limited number of states in 1976, it was necessary to attempt to exclude these credit hours from the continuing education hours measure. For this reason, hours for 93 practitioners who reported more than 50 hours of credit in 1976 were recoded as "50 hours." This change reduced the mean from 24.79 to 21.51 and the standard deviation from 24.45 to 14.11. Both the original and recoded continuing education hours were tested in the following analyses, with similar results.

Chapter 6

1. When entered before quality measures, professionalism accounts for 20 percent of the variance and quality accounts for 4 percent. There is no theoretical justification for entering the variables in that order, however.

2. Strictly speaking, it is not appropriate to hold constant the volume of services since quality improvements generally will decrease the volume of services and cause higher prices. Exclusion of the measures of volume from the table 6.5 regression has little impact, however, so the table 6.6 results are reported for convenience.

3. The continuing education requirement is *not* present in only seven states, in which 170 survey respondents, or 14 percent of the sample, practice. The measure isolates a small and possibly "extreme" group of states and its strong effect may reflect other unmeasured factors (for instance, an extremely "commercial" environment in New York, in which 80 of the 170 respondents practice).

References

Abrams, Richard A.
1978
"Denturism and the Dentists." New England Journal of Medicine 299 (November 16): 1131–1133.

Akers, Ronald L.
1968
"The Professional Association and the Legal Regulation of Practice." Law and Society Review 2 (May): 463–482.

Akers, Ronald L., and Richard Quinney
1968
"Differential Organization of Health Professions: A Comparative Analysis." American Sociological Review 33 (February): 104–121.

American Optometric Association
1966
Manual of Professional Practice for the American Optometrist. St. Louis: American Optometric Association.
1971
Optometry Today: The Vision Care Profession. St. Louis: American Optometric Association. 31 pp.
1974
Compilation of State Board Rules and Regulations. St. Louis: American Optometric Association. Unpaginated.
1976a
"Listing of States Prohibiting or Allowing Optometrist and/or Optician Price Advertising as of January 1, 1976." St. Louis: American Optometric Association. Mimeo, 2 pp.
1976b
"Membership Count for June, 1976 as of July 6, 1976." St. Louis: American Optometric Association. Mimeo, 1 p.
1976c
Membership names and addresses as of 10/14/76. St. Louis: American Optometric Association. Computer printout, 558 pp.
1976d
1975–1976 Annual Report. St. Louis: American Optometric Association. Unpaginated.
1977
"Advertising, Cost Issues Confronted by Optometry." Annual Report 1976–77. St. Louis: American Optometric Association. Unpaginated.

1978
"Wisconsin Legislation." Bulletin from Counsel, Vol. 36, Bulletin No. 35, May 10. St. Louis: American Optometric Association.
1979
"Nebraska Legislation." Bulletin from Counsel, Vol. 37, Bulletin No. 35, February 14. St. Louis: American Optometric Association.

American Optometric Association News
1975a
"Debunking Benham: A Critique." American Optometric Association News 14 (October 1): 5.
1975b
"Economist Lee Benham: More Academician than Activist." American Optometric Association News 14 (November 1).
1976
"Optometric Mean Net Income Rises to $33,319." American Optometric Association News 15 (September 15): 1, 6.

American Pharmaceutical Association
1975
"American Pharmaceutical Association Comment to the Federal Trade Commission on Prescription Price Disclosure." November 21. Washington, D.C.: American Pharmaceutical Association. 10 pp.

Ancone, Peter
1976
"Advertising Debate Draws to a Close." Optical Journal and Review of Optometry 113 (November): 48–56.

Arnould, Richard J., and Thomas S. Friedland
1977
"The Effect of Fee Schedules on the Legal Services Industry." Journal of Human Resources 12 (Spring): 258–265.

Aron, Farrell D.
1974
"Results of the 1974 AOA Opinion Poll and Economic Survey." Journal of the American Optometric Association 45 (December): 1395–1401.
1976
Statement before the Federal Trade Commission, San Francisco, July 30. St. Louis: American Optometric Association. Mimeo, 16 pp.

Avellone, Joseph C., and Francis D. Moore
1978
"The Federal Trade Commission Enters a New Arena: Health Services." New England Journal of Medicine 299 (August 31): 478–483.

Baughcum, Alan
1976
A Legal and Economic Survey of N.C. Occupational Licensing Boards. Raleigh, N.C.: Office of the Attorney General. Mimeo, 51 pp.

Beales, J. Howard
1980
"The Economics of Regulating the Professions." Pp. 125–142 in Roger D. Blair and Stephen Rubin (eds.), Regulating the Professions. Lexington: D. C. Heath.

Becker, Howard S.
1970
"The Nature of a Profession." Pp. 87–103 in Sociological Work. Chicago: Aldine.

Begun, James W.
1979
"The Consequences of Professionalization for Health Services Delivery: Evidence from Optometry." Journal of Health and Social Behavior 20 (December): 376–386.

Begun, James W., and Roger D. Feldman
1979
A Social and Economic Analysis of Professional Regulation in Optometry. Final Report, Grant No. 1–R01–HS–03085–01, National Center for Health Services Research, Department of Health, Education and Welfare.

Begun, James W., and Ronald C. Lippincott
1980
"The Politics of Professional Control." In Julius Roth (ed.), Research in the Sociology of Health Care. Greenwich, Connecticut: JAI Press, forthcoming.

Bell, Bill D., and Jacquelyn K. Bell
1972
"Professionalism as a Multidimensional Perspective." American Journal of Occupational Therapy 8 (November-December): 391–398.

Benham, Lee
1972
"The Effects of Advertising on the Price of Eyeglasses." Journal of Law and Economics 15 (October): 337–352.
1976
Personal communication. Breakdown of eyeglass price by state, 1970.
1978
"Guilds and the Form of Competition in the Health Care Sector." Pp. 453–467 in Warren Greenberg (ed.), Competition in the Health Care Sector: Past, Present, and Future. Washington, D.C.: Government Printing Office.

Benham, Lee, and Alexandra Benham
1975
"Regulating Through the Professions: A Perspective on Information Control." Journal of Law and Economics 18 (October): 421–447.

Bennett, Irving
1976
"The Case *Against* Price Advertising." Optometric Management 12 (August): 75–79.

Berlant, Jeffrey L.
1975
Profession and Monopoly: A Study of Medicine in the United States and Great Britain. Berkeley: University of California Press.

Bernstein, Arthur H.
1977
"Licensing of Health Care Personnel." Hospitals 51 (August 1): 106, 108, 110, 113.

Bledstein, Burton J.
1976
The Culture of Professionalism. New York: W. W. Norton.

Bridgstock, Martin
1976
"Professions and Social Background: The Work Organization of General Practitioners." Sociological Review 24 (May): 309–329.

Bucher, Rue
1962
"Pathology: A Study of Social Movements within a Profession." Social Problems 10 (Summer): 40–51.

Bucher, Rue, and Anselm Strauss
1961
"Professions in Process." American Journal of Sociology 66 (January): 325–334.

Carr-Saunders, A. M.
1928
"Professionalization in Historical Perspective." Pp. 3–9 in Howard M. Vollmer and Donald L. Mills (eds.), Professionalization. Englewood Cliffs: Prentice-Hall, 1966.

Carroll, Sidney L., and Robert J. Gaston
1977
Occupational Licensing. Final Report, National Science Foundation Grant APR75-16792, September 15, 1975–August 31, 1977.

Challenor, Bernard
1978
"Optometry in the Hospital: A Cooperative Endeavor." American Journal of Public Health 68 (April): 325.

Clarkson, Kenneth W., and Timothy J. Muris
1979
"The Federal Trade Commission and Occupational Regulation." Draft paper presented to the American Enterprise Institute Conference on Occupational Licensure and Regulation, Washington, D.C., February 22–23. Mimeo, 51 pp. Cited with permission.

Coate, Douglas
1974
Studies in the Economics of the Profession of Optometry. Unpublished Ph.D. dissertation, City University of New York.

Cohen, Harris S.
1973a
"Professional Licensure, Organizational Behavior, and the Public Interest." Milbank Memorial Fund Quarterly 51 (Winter): 73–93.
1973b
"State Licensing Boards and Quality Assurance: A New Approach to an Old Problem." Pp. 49–65 in the U.S. Department of Health, Education and Welfare, Quality Assurance of Medical Care. DHEW Publication No. (HSM) 73–2021. Washington, D.C.: Government Printing Office.

Cohen, Harris S., and Lawrence H. Miike
1974
"Toward a More Responsive System of Professional Licensure." International Journal of Health Services 4 (Spring): 265–272.

Corbett, John E.
1940
"Think It Over." Journal of the American Optometric Association 11 (May): 229–301.

Council of State Governments
1979
State Regulatory Policies: Dentistry and the Health Professions. Lexington, Ky: Council of State Governments.

Daynard, Matthew, Ralph E. Stone, and Ronald W. Phelon
1979
"Remarks Presented at the U.S. Public Health Service Region IX Dental Conference." August 31, Pacific Grove, California. Mimeo, 16 pp.

Derbyshire, Robert C.
1974
"Medical Ethics and Discipline." Journal of the American Medical Association 228 (April 1): 59–62.

Dolan, Andrew K.
1978
"The New York State Nurses Association 1985 Proposal: Who Needs It." Journal of Health Politics, Policy and Law 2 (Winter): 508–530.
1980
"Occupational Licensure and Obstruction of Change in the Health Care Delivery System: Some Recent Developments." Pp. 223–244 in Roger D. Blair and Stephen Rubin (eds.), Regulating the Professions. Lexington: D. C. Heath.

Donabedian, Avedis
1978
Needed Research in the Assessment and Monitoring of the Quality of Medical Care. DHEW Publication No. (PHS) 78–3219. Washington, D.C.: National Center for Health Services Research.

Durkheim, Emile
1902
"Some Notes on Occupational Groups." Preface to the second edition of George Simpson (trans.), The Division of Labor in Society. New York: Free Press, 1933.

Egdahl, Richard M., and Paul M. Gertman (eds.)
1976
Quality Assurance in Health Care. Germantown, Md.: Aspen Systems.

Eger, Milton J.
1975
"Price Advertising and Consumerism." Journal of the American Optometric Association 46 (June): 579–581.

Ellwood, Paul M., Jr., Patrick O'Donoghue, Walter McClure, Robert Holley, Rick J. Carlson, and Earl Hoagberg
1973
Assuring the Quality of Health Care. Minneapolis: Interstudy.

Enterline, P. E., J. C. McDonald, A. D. McDonald, L. Davignon, and V. Salter
1973
"Effects of 'Free' Medical Care on Medical Practice—The Quebec Experience." New England Journal of Medicine 288 (May 31): 1152–1155.

Etzioni, Amitai
1974
"PSRO: A Poor Mechanism and a Possible Alternative." American Journal of Public Health 64 (May): 415, 507–508.

Evans, Robert G.
1974
"Supplier-Induced Demand: Some Empirical Evidence and Implications." Pp. 162–173 in Mark Perlman (ed.), The Economics of Health and Medical Care. New York: John Wiley and Sons.

Fair, Ron G.
1977
"Statement by Ron G. Fair, O.D. on Behalf of the American Optometric Association before the Subcommittee on Monopoly of the Senate Committee on Small Business." May 26. Mimeo, 12 pp.

Federal Register
1978
"Advertising of Ophthalmic Goods and Services." Federal Register 43 (June 2): 23992–24008.

Federal Trade Commission News
1979a
"Professional Licensing Used as Means to Limit Competition, FTC Chairman Says." FTC News, February 22.
1979b
"FTC Consent Order Would Curb Restrictions on Dental Advertising, Apply AMA Case Result to Dentists." FTC News, April 29.

Federation of Associations of Health Regulatory Boards
1976
Statement Regarding the HEW Publication "A Proposal for Credentialing Health Manpower." Appendix A. Chicago: FAHRB. Mimeo, 65 pp.

Feldman, Roger
1979
"Price and Quality Differences in the Physicians' Services Market." Southern Economic Journal 45 (January): 885–891.

Feldman, Roger, and James W. Begun
1978
"The Effects of Advertising: Lessons from Optometry." Journal of Human Resources 13 (Supplement): 247–262.
1980
"Does Advertising of Prices Reduce the Mean and Variance of Prices?" Economic Inquiry 18 (July): 487–492.

Feldstein, Paul J.
1977
Health Associations and the Demand for Legislation: The Political Economy of Health. Cambridge: Ballinger.

Frech, H. E.
1974
"Occupational Licensure and Health Care Productivity: The Issues and the Literature." Pp. 119–139 in John Rafferty (ed.), Health Manpower and Productivity: The Literature and Required Future Research. Lexington: D. C. Heath.

Freidson, Eliot
1970a
Profession of Medicine. New York: Dodd, Mead.
1970b
Professional Dominance. New York: Atherton.

Geist, Robert W.
1978
"Advertising in Medicine—A Physician's Perspective." New England Journal of Medicine 299 (August 31): 483–486.

Gilb, Corrine L.
1966
Hidden Hierarchies. New York: Harper and Row.

Glazier, Nathan
1978
"The Attack on the Professions." Commentary 65 (November): 34–41.

Goldman, Fred, and Michael Grossman
1978
"The Demand for Pediatric Care: An Hedonic Approach." Journal of Political Economy 86 (April): 259–280.

Goode, William J.
1960
"Encroachment, Charlatanism and the Emerging Professions: Psychology, Sociology and Medicine." American Sociological Review 25 (December): 902–914.

Greenberg, Warren (ed.)
1978
Competition in the Health Care Sector: Past, Present, and Future. Bureau of Economics, U.S. Federal Trade Commission. Washington, D.C.: Government Printing Office.

Greenwood, Ernest
1966
"The Elements of Professionalization." Pp. 10–19 in Howard M. Vollmer and Donald L. Mills (eds.), Professionalization. Englewood Cliffs: Prentice-Hall.

Gregg, James R.
1965
The Story of Optometry. New York: Ronald Press.
1972
American Optometric Association: A History. St. Louis: American Optometric Association.

Haffner, Alden N.
1971
A National Study of Assisting Manpower in Optometry. Springfield, Virginia: National Technical Information Service.
1976
"Problems Behind the Problem." Optometric Weekly 67 (June 3): 21–26.
1977
"The Legislative Inquiries—Some Issues and Some Answers." Optometric Weekly 68 (December 8): 9–12, 14–15, 43–46.

Hall, Richard H.
1968
"Professionalization and Bureaucratization." American Sociological Review 33 (February): 92–104.
1979
"The Social Construction of the Professions." Sociology of Work and Occupations 6 (February): 124–126.

Halmos, Paul (ed.)
1973
Professionalization and Social Change. Sociological Review Monograph 20. Keele, Great Britain: University of Keele.

Halstead, John P.
1975
Examining the Examiners. Tallahassee, Florida: Committee on Regulated Industries and Licensing, Florida House of Representatives.

Havighurst, Clark C.
1977a
"Controlling Health Care Costs." Journal of Health Politics, Policy and Law 1 (Winter): 471–498.
1977b
"The Ethics of Cost Control in Medical Care." Soundings 60 (Spring): 22–39.

Havighurst, Clark C., and Philip C. Kissam
1979
"The Antitrust Implications of Relative Value Scales in Medicine." Journal
of Health Politics, Policy and Law 4 (Spring): 48–86.

Hayes, Michael T.
1978
"The Semi-Sovereign Pressure Groups: A Critique of Current Theory and
an Alternative Typology." Journal of Politics 40 (February): 134–161.

Hazell, B. Woodward
1934
"Problem of Making Optometry a Fully Recognized Profession." Optical
Journal and Review of Optometry 71 (April 1): 22, 26.
1938
"Trends and Prophecies in Optometric Education." Optical Journal and
Review of Optometry 75 (April 15): 16–17, 42.

Hershey, Nathan
1976
"Institutional Licensure for Health Professionals?" Hospital Progress 57
(September): 75–80.

Hirsch, Monroe J., and Ralph E. Wick
1968
The Optometric Profession. Philadelphia: Chilton.

Hofstetter, H. W.
1948
Optometry: Professional, Economic, and Legal Aspects. St. Louis: C. V.
Mosby.

Holen, Arlene S.
1965
"Effects of Professional Licensing Arrangements on Interstate Labor
Mobility and Resource Allocation." Journal of Political Economy 73 (Octo-
ber): 492–498.
1977
The Economics of Dental Licensing. Arlington, Va: Center for Naval
Analysis. NTIS Report Number HRP-0900163.

Horowitz, Ira
1980
"The Economic Foundations of Self-Regulation in the Professions." Pp.
3–28 in Roger D. Blair and Stephen Rubin (eds.), Regulating the Professions. Lexington: D. C. Heath.

Hubbard, Bruce
1977
"Ad Hoc Committee of Health Professions and Related Organizations."
Pp. 25–27 in Report on the Third National Administrative and Legal
Forum for State Health Regulatory Boards, September 17–19, 1976. Chica-
go: Federation of Associations of Health Regulatory Boards.

Ingelfinger, F. J.
1976
"Deprofessionalizing the Profession." New England Journal of Medicine
294 (February 5): 334–335.

Institute of Medicine
1976
Assessing Quality in Health Care: An Evaluation. Washington, D.C.:
National Academy of Sciences.

International Association of Boards of Examiners in Optometry
1974
Proceedings of the 55th Annual Meeting, June 15, 16, 1974. Wallace, N.C.:
International Association of Boards of Examiners in Optometry.
1975
Proceedings of the 56th Annual Meeting, June 14, 15, 1975. Wallace, N.C.:
International Association of Boards of Examiners in Optometry.
1976
Proceedings of the 57th Annual Meeting, June 19–20, 1976. Wallace, N.C.:
International Association of Boards of Examiners in Optometry.

Journal of the Florida Optometric Association
1954
"Call to Arms Sounded by AOA President Wahl." Journal of the Florida
Optometric Association 19 (January-February): 3, 11.

Kessel, Reuben A.
1970
"The AMA and the Supply of Physicians." Law and Contemporary Problems 35 (Spring): 267–282.

Ketchum, William M.
1939
"Is Optometry a Trade or a Profession?" Journal of the American
Optometric Association 11 (December): 142–143.

Klegon, Douglas
1978
"The Sociology of Professions: An Emerging Perspective." Sociology of
Work and Occupations 5 (August): 259–283

Kraft, P., and G. M. Weinberg
1975
"Professionalization of Programming." Datamation 21 (October): 169–172.

Krevans, Julius R.
1979
"The FTC and the Profession of Medicine." Journal of Medical Education 54 (April): 344–346.

Larson, Magali Sarfatti
1977
The Rise of Professionalism. Berkeley: University of California Press.

Leffler, Keith B.
1978
"Physician Licensure: Competition and Monopoly in American Medicine." Journal of Law and Economics 21 (April): 165–186.

Leland, Hayne E.
1979
"Quacks, Lemons, and Licensing: A Theory of Minimum Quality Standards." Journal of Political Economy 87 (December): 1328–1346.

LeMaitre, George D.
1974
"PSRO as a Threat to Confidentiality." Letter to the editor, New England Journal of Medicine 290 (June 6): 1323.

Lipscomb, Joseph
1977
"Legal Restrictions on Input Substitution in Production: The Case of General Dentistry." Working Paper #3771, Institute of Policy Sciences and Public Affairs, Duke University. 39 pp.

MacRae, Duncan, Jr.
1976
The Social Function of Social Science. New Haven: Yale University Press.
1977
"Professions and Social Sciences as Sources of Public Values." Soundings 60 (Spring): 1–21.

Martin, Donald L.
1979
"Will the Sun Set on Occupational Licensing?" Draft paper presented to the American Enterprise Institute Conference on Occupational Licensure and Regulation, Washington, D.C., February 22–23. Mimeo, 23 pp. Cited with permission.

Maurizi, Alex R.

1974

"Occupational Licensing and the Public Interest." Journal of Political Economy 83 (March–April): 399–413.

1979

"The Impact of Regulation on Quality: The Case of California Contractors." Draft paper presented to the American Enterprise Institute Conference on Occupational Licensure and Regulation, Washington, D.C., February 22–23. Mimeo, 22 pp. Cited with permission.

Medical World News

1974a

"Thunder from Medicine's Right Wing." Medical World News 15 (June 21): 38–44.

1974b

"How Well Does Medicine Police Itself?" Medical World News 15 (March 15): 62–72.

Merton, Robert K.

1958

"The Functions of the Professional Association." American Journal of Nursing 58 (January): 50–54.

Moore, Thomas G.

1961

"The Purpose of Licensing." Journal of Law and Economics 4 (October): 93–117.

Moore, Wilbert E.

1970

The Professions: Rules and Roles. New York: Russell Sage Foundation.

Nicolais, John P.

1976

"Policy Development and Strategy in the Licensure of Speech Pathologists and Audiologists." American Journal of Occupational Therapy 30 (January): 21–26.

Niemann, Larry

1978

"Motion to Affirm or Dismiss Filed by Appellee Texas Optometric Association, Inc." No. 77–1164 in the Supreme Court of the United States, October Term, 1977. Dr. N. Jay Rogers, O.D. and W. J. Dickinson v. Dr. E. Richard Friedman, O.D. et al. March 20. 40 pp.

North Carolina Governmental Evaluation Commission

1979a

Staff Report on North Carolina State Board of Dental Examiners. Raleigh, N.C.

1979b
Staff Report on North Carolina State Board of Examiners in Optometry.
Raleigh, N.C.
1979c
Staff Report on North Carolina State Board of Opticians. Raleigh, N.C.

Nunnally, Jum C.
1967
Psychometric Theory. New York: McGraw-Hill.

Olson, Mancur
1965
The Logic of Collective Action. Cambridge: Harvard University Press.

Optical Journal and Review of Optometry
1922
"Why Optometry Is a Profession." Optical Journal and Review of
Optometry 49 (June 29): 33–34.
1976
"Rx for an Eye Care Partnership." Optical Journal and Review of
Optometry 113 (October): 35–44.

Optometric Manpower Resources Project
1976
Optometric Manpower Resources 1973. Washington, D.C.: Optometric
Manpower Resources Project. Mimeo, 159 pp.

Optometric Weekly
1977
"Price Advertising and the Implications for Optometry." Optometric
Weekly 68 (January 27): 90–93.

Orzack, Louis H., and Lester A. Janoff
1976
"Sociological Perspectives on the Profession of Optometry: A New Look at
Trends Since 1958." American Journal of Optometry and Physiological
Optics 53 (May): 259–269.

Orzack, Louis H., and John R. Uglum
1958
"Sociological Perspectives on the Profession of Optometry." American
Journal of Optometry 35 (August): 407–424.

Pace, Loren L.
1975
"Dr. Pace on Dr. Benham." Letter to the editor of the American
Optometric Association News 14 (December 15): 4.

Palmer, Alan K.
1979
"Regulation, Professional Responsibility, and Market Forces in the Health Care Field." Journal of Medical Education 54 (April): 275–283.

Parsons, Talcott
1968
"Professions." Pp. 536–547 in David L. Sills (ed.), International Encyclopedia of the Social Sciences, vol. 12. New York: The Macmillan Company and the Free Press.

The PEN
1980
"California Order Threatens Quality Hospital Care." The PEN 4 (January 1): 8.

Percy, Charles
1975
"FTC Launches Investigation of Eyeglass Advertising Restrictions." Congressional Record—Senate 123 (September 24): 16654–16655.

Pfeffer, Jeffrey
1974a
"Administrative Regulation and Licensing: Social Problem or Solution?" Social Problems 21 (April): 468–479.
1974b
"Some Evidence on Occupational Licensing and Occupational Incomes." Social Forces 53 (September): 102–111.

Posner, Richard A.
1974
"Theories of Economic Regulation." Bell Journal of Economics and Management Science 5 (Autumn): 335–358.

Professional Press, Inc.
1976
The Blue Book of Optometrists. Chicago: Professional Press.

Rayack, Elton
1976
An Economic Analysis of Occupational Licensure. Report to the U.S. Department of Labor, Grant No. 98-02-6851. Mimeo, 165 pp.

Relman, Arnold S.
1978
"Professional Directories—But Not Commercial Advertising—As a Public Service." New England Journal of Medicine 299 (August 31): 476–478.

Reynolds, James A.
1976
"How Soon Will Your Colleagues Begin Advertising?" Medical Economics 53 (February 23): 31–40.

Ritzer, George
1977
Working: Conflict and Change. Englewood Cliffs, N.J.: Prentice-Hall.

Roemer, Ruth
1971
"Legal Regulation of Health Manpower in the 1970's: Needs, Objectives, Options, Constraints, and Their Trade-Offs." Pp. 33–51 in Health Manpower: Adapting in the Seventies, Report of the 1971 National Health Forum. New York: National Health Council.

Rootman, Irving, and Donald L. Mills
1974
"Professional Behavior of American and Canadian Chiropractors." Journal of Health and Social Behavior 15 (March): 3–12.

Rose, David L.
1977
"Proposed Equal Employment Opportunity Commission Guidelines." Pp. 21–23 in Report on the Third National Administrative and Legal Forum for State Health Regulatory Boards, September 17–19, 1976. Chicago: Federation of Associations of Health Regulatory Boards.

Roth, Julius A.
1974
"Professionalism: The Sociologist's Decoy." Sociology of Work and Occupations 1 (February): 6–23.

Rubin, Stephen
1980
"The Legal Web of Professional Regulation." Pp. 29–60 in Roger D. Blair and Stephen Rubin (eds.), Regulating the Professions. Lexington: D. C. Heath.

RxO Journal of Opticianry
1975
"Perspective on Eyeglass Advertising." RxO Journal of Opticianry 26 (November-December): 24, 26.

Salisbury, Robert, and John Heinz
1970
"A Theory of Policy Analysis and Some Preliminary Applications." Pp. 39–60 in Ira Sharkansky (ed.), Policy Analysis in Political Science. Chicago: Markham.

Shannon, B. J.

1975a

"AOA President Attacks Price Advertising." Optometric Weekly 66 (April 3): 284–290.

1975b

"Mutual Interests of Optometrists and Pharmacists." American Pharmaceutical Association Journal 15 (October): 554–555, 598–599.

Sheard, Charles

1939

"A Program for Professional Optometry." Optical Journal and Review of Optometry 76 (June 1): 18–21.

Shimberg, Benjamin

1979

"Promoting Regulatory Reform: The Case of Occupational Licensing." Paper presented to the Symposium on Regulatory Policy, Chicago, Illinois, December 3–4, 1979. Mimeo, 20 pp.

Shimberg, Benjamin, Barbara F. Esser, and Daniel H. Kruger

1973

Occupational Licensing: Practices and Policies. Washington, D.C.: Public Affairs Press.

Simpson, Richard L.

1971

"Imperative Control, Associationalism, and the Moral Order." Pp. 253–271 in Herman Turk and Richard L. Simpson (eds.), Institutions and Social Exchange. Indianapolis: Bobbs-Merrill.

Sims, Joseph

1975

"State Regulation and Federal Antitrust Laws: The Justice Department's View of Licensing." Paper presented to the National Council on Occupational Licensing, Inc., August 4, Virginia Beach, Virginia. Mimeo, 14 pp.

1978

"Antitrust and Medicine: A Justice Department Perspective." Group Practice 27 (May-June): 8–10.

Sloan, Frank A., and John H. Lorant

1976

"The Allocation of Physicians' Services: Evidence on Length-of-Visit." Quarterly Review of Economics and Business 16 (Autumn): 85–103.

Snizek, William E.

1972

"Hall's Professionalism Scale: An Empirical Reassessment." American Sociological Review 37 (February): 109–114.

Southern Research Institute
1976
"The Advertising of Ophthalmic Goods and Services: An Economic and Statistical Review of Selected FTC and Related Documents. Report to American Optometric Association." Birmingham: Southern Research Institute. Mimeo, 39 pp.

Spencer, Herbert
1896
The Principles of Sociology, Vol. II–3. New York: D. Appleton.

Stern, D. N., and D. R. Klock
1975
"Public Policy and Professionalization of Life Underwriters." American Business Law Journal 13 (Fall): 225–238.

Stigler, George
1971
"The Theory of Economic Regulation." Bell Journal of Economics and Management Science 2 (Spring): 3–21.

Stock, Frederick
1978
"Professional Advertising." American Journal of Public Health 68 (December): 1207–1209.

Thelan, Gil
1977
"FTC Looking at Eyeglass Industry." Chicago Daily News, February 9, pp. 27–28.

Tiffen, Judith
1976
"An Historical Perspective on Regulation of the Vision Care Industry." Hearing Exhibit 264, Trade Regulation Rule on the Advertising of Ophthalmic Goods and Services, July 28. Washington, D.C.: Federal Trade Commission. 24 pp.

Timperly, Stuart R., and Michael D. Osbaldeston
1975
"The Professionalization Process." Sociological Review 23 (August): 607–627.

Topaz, Peter M.
1977
"Guilty until Proven Innocent!—News of the On-going Trial of Optometry." Optometric Weekly 68 (February 10).

Trapnell, Gordon R., Consulting Actuaries
1976
The Impact of National Health Insurance on the Use and Spending for Sight Correction Services. Falls Church, Virginia: Gordon R. Trapnell Consulting Actuaries.

Truman, David B.
1962
The Governmental Process. New York: Knopf.

Tuohy, Carolyn J.
1976
"Private Government, Property, and Professionalism." Canadian Journal of Political Science 9 (December): 668–681.

Turville, A. E.
1920
"Extreme View as to Requirements for Making Optometry Strictly Professional." Optical Journal and Review of Optometry 46 (October 14): 1095.

U.S. Bureau of the Census
1973
County and City Data Book, 1972. Washington, D.C.: Government Printing Office.

U.S. Department of Health, Education and Welfare
1970
Health Resources Statistics. PHS Publ. No. 1509. Washington, D.C.: Government Printing Office.
1972
"Legislative History of Professional Standards Review Organization Provisions of the Social Security Act Amendments." Office of the Secretary, Department of Health, Education and Welfare. Mimeo, 38 pp.
1976a
Health Resources Statistics, 1975. DHEW Publ. No. (HRA) 76–1509. Washington, D.C.: Government Printing Office.
1976b
A Proposal for Credentialing Health Manpower. Washington, D.C.: Subcommittee on Health Manpower Credentialing, Health Resources Administration. 22 pp.
1977
State Regulation of Health Manpower. DHEW Publ. No. (HRA) 77–49. Washington, D.C.: Government Printing Office.
1979
Health Resources Statistics, 1976–77. DHEW Publ. No. (PHS) 79–1509. Washington, D.C.: Government Printing Office.

U.S. Federal Trade Commission
1975
Prescription Drug Price Disclosures. Staff Report to the Federal Trade Commission. Washington, D.C.: Federal Trade Commission.
1976a
Advertising of Ophthalmic Goods and Services. Washington, D.C.: Division of Special Projects, Bureau of Consumer Protection, Federal Trade Commission.
1976b
Report of the Presiding Officer on Proposed Trade Regulation Rule Regarding Advertising of Ophthalmic Goods and Services. Public Record 215–52. Washington, D.C.: Federal Trade Commission.
1979
Health Services Policy Session. Edited version. Washington, D.C.: Federal Trade Commission.

U.S. General Accounting Office
1980
Increased Use of Expanded Function Dental Auxiliaries Would Benefit Consumers, Dentists, and Taxpayers. HRD-80-51. Washington, D.C.: Government Printing Office.

U.S. Senate
1977
Restrictive and Anticompetitive Practices in the Eyeglass Industry. Subcommittee on Monopoly and Anticompetitive Practices, Select Committee on Small Business. Stock No. 052–070–04183–8. Washington, D.C.: Government Printing Office.

Wall Street Journal
1976
"Reexamination of State Licensing Boards Urged by New Head of Antitrust Division." Wall Street Journal, September 16, p. 4.

Walsh, James L., and Ray H. Elling
1968
"Professionalism and the Poor—Structural Effects and Professional Behavior." Journal of Health and Social Behavior 9 (March): 16–28.

Wardwell, Walter I.
1963
"Limited, Marginal, and Quasi-Practitioners." Pp. 213–239 in H. E. Freeman, S. Levine, and L. G. Reeder (eds.), Handbook of Medical Sociology. Englewood Cliffs: Prentice-Hall.

Webster, George D.
1976
"Professional Societies Take a New Look at Bans on Advertising." Association Management 28 (April): 30–32.

Weinthal, D. S., and G. J. O'Keefe
1974
"Professionalism among Broadcast Newsmen in an Urban Area." Journal of Broadcasting 18 (Spring): 193–209.

White, William D.
1979
Public Health and Private Gain: The Economics of Licensing Clinical Laboratory Personnel. Chicago: Maaroufa Press.

Wickersham, J. A.
1952
"The Philosophy of Professionalism." Colorado Optometrist (June): 16–17.

Wilensky, Harold L.
1964
"The Professionalization of Everyone?" American Journal of Sociology 70 (September): 137–158.

Zelizer, V. A., and G. L. Zelizer
1973
"Conservative Rabbinate—Quest of Professionalism." Judaism 22 (Fall): 490–496.

Zimmerman, Thomas F.
1974
"Is Professionalization the Answer to Improving Health Care?" American Journal of Occupational Therapy 28 (September): 465–468.

Index

www.ingramcontent.com/pod-product-compliance
Lightning Source LLC
Chambersburg PA
CBHW050529270326
41926CB00015B/3146